# Contents

# Puerto Rican Shortbread Cookies

**MAKES: 20 cookies | PREP TIME: 10 minutes | COOK TIME: 25 minutes**

**Ingredients**

- ½ cup (1 stick) butter
- ½ cup shortening
- ½ cup granulated sugar
- 1 beaten egg yolk
- 1 teaspoon vanilla
- Salt
- 2¼ cups flour
- 1 (10-ounce) can guava paste

**Directions**

**Step 1**

Preheat your oven to 350°F. In a large bowl cream together the butter, shortening, and sugar, and egg yolk until it starts to form peaks. Mix in vanilla, salt, and flour until completely combined.

**Step 2**

Scoop about 1 tablespoon of dough at a time onto a parchment-lined baking sheet. Press your thumb into the center of the cookie to create an indent, and place about ½-inch cube of guava paste into each indent. Bake for 20 to 25 minutes. Remove from oven and place cookies on a wire rack to cool before serving.

VARIATION TIP: Instead of guava paste, you can use just about any jelly you like.

# Three Milks Cake

**MAKES: 12 servings | PREP TIME: 25 minutes | COOK TIME: 45 minutes plus 1 hour chill time**

**Ingredients**

- 5 eggs, yolks and whites separated
- 1 cup granulated sugar
- 1 teaspoon vanilla
- 1¼ cups flour
- ¾ teaspoon salt
- 1 teaspoon baking powder
- 1 (12-ounce) can evaporated milk
- 1 (14-ounce) can sweetened condensed milk
- ¼ cup whole milk
- 1½ cup whipped cream

- 1 tablespoon powdered sugar

**Directions**

**Step 1**

Preheat your oven to 350°F. In a small bowl, beat egg yolks until they become light and fluffy. Add sugar and vanilla and mix until combined.

**Step 2**

In a separate bowl, beat the egg whites until they form peaks (you may want to use an electric mixer for this). Fold whites into the yolks with a spatula, then slowly fold the flour, salt, and baking powder into the mixture.

**Step 3**

Pour batter into a greased and floured 9-by-13-inch baking dish, and bake for 35 to 40 minutes. Test cake with a toothpick to make sure it is done. Remove cake from oven and allow to cool completely.

**Step 4**

In a medium bowl whisk together the three milks. Using a small wooden skewer, poke holes in the cake and pour the milk mixture over the whole cake. Place the cake in the refrigerator for at least 1 hour to chill.

5 . Once chilled, in a small bowl beat together the whipped cream and powdered sugar. Spread the mixture over the cake before serving.

VARIATION TIP: For a real island taste, replace the sweetened condensed milk with coconut cream, usually found in the canned goods aisle of most grocery stores.

# Sweet Potato Pudding

**MAKES: 10 servings | PREP TIME: 15 minutes | COOK TIME: 1 hour 25 minutes**

**Ingredients**

- 1½ pounds sweet potatoes
- 1½ pounds pumpkin
- Water
- 1½ teaspoons salt
- 1 cup coconut milk
- 1½ cup granulated sugar
- ½ teaspoon ground cloves
- ½ teaspoon cinnamon
- ½ teaspoon ginger
- ¼ cup rice flour
- 3 beaten eggs

**Directions**

**Step 1**

Preheat your oven to 350°F. Peel the pumpkin and sweet potatoes and cut into 2-inch cubes. Bring a large pot of water to boil, enough to cover the pumpkin and sweet potatoes, and boil for about 20 minutes.

**Step 2**

Drain the water. Put pumpkin and sweet potatoes in a large bowl with the salt, coconut milk, sugar, ground cloves, cinnamon, ginger, flour, and eggs, and beat with a mixer until smooth and incorporated.

**Step 3**

Pour the batter into a greased 8-by-8-inch baking dish. Bake for 1 hour.

**Step 4**

Remove from the oven, turn the broiler on, and place under the broiler for about 2 minutes so it gets a nice crust on it. Once done baking, place in the refrigerator to cool before serving.

VARIATION TIP: Classically this recipe is made with Calabasa (a caribbean squash) rather than pumpkin. Calabasas can be hard to find sometimes so I use pumpkin, but if you can find them use those instead.

# Rum Cake

**MAKES: 8 servings | PREP TIME: 10 minutes | COOK TIME: 1 hour**

Rum cake is a popular dessert no matter where you go. In Puerto Rico it's usually enjoyed as a holiday treat. The Puerto Rican version, *Bizcochos de Ron* , not only has rum in the batter but it's also typically soaked in rum glaze as well.

**Ingredients**

FOR THE CAKE

- ½ cup chopped pecans
- 1 (18½-ounce) box yellow cake mix
- 1 (3¼-ounce) box instant vanilla pudding
- ½ cup dark rum
- ½ cup vegetable oil
- 4 eggs

FOR THE RUM GLAZE

- 1 cup granulated sugar
- ½ cup (1 stick) butter
- ¼ cup dark rum
- ¼ cup water

TO MAKE THE CAKE

**Directions**

**Step 1**

Preheat your oven to 350°F. Grease a Bundt pan, then sprinkle the chopped pecans across the bottom of the pan.

**Step 2**

In a large bowl beat together the cake mix, vanilla pudding, rum, oil, and eggs until completely combined. Pour cake batter into prepared Bundt pan over the pecans, place in the oven, and bake for one hour.

TO MAKE THE GLAZE

**Directions**

**Step 1**

About 10 minutes before the cake is finished baking, mix together the sugar, butter, rum, and water in a small saucepan. Bring to a boil, then turn down the heat and simmer for 3 to 4 minutes, stirring constantly.

**Step 2**

Test cake with a toothpick to make sure it's done, then remove from the oven. Invert the pan and slide the cake out onto a serving plate. Pour the hot glaze over the cake and allow it to soak in and cool before serving.

VARIATION TIP: If you like raisins you can add them into this recipe. Soak the raisins in rum for at least a day before mixing them into the batter.

# Pickled Plantains

**MAKES: 4 servings | PREP TIME: 4 hours | COOK TIME: 4 hours**

**Ingredients**

- 1 red onion, sliced
- 6 garlic cloves, minced
- 2 cups olive oil
- 1 cup apple cider vinegar
- ½ cup alcaparrado
- ½ teaspoon peppercorns
- 10 green bananas
- 1 avocado, diced

**Directions**

**Step 1**

Put sliced onion, garlic, olive oil, apple cider vinegar, alcaparrado, and peppercorns into the slow cooker and stir. Set cooker to high and cook for 3 hours. (This is a good "set and forget" recipe, giving you time to do other things while the ingredients are pickling.)

**Step 2**

Cut the ends off of the bananas. Sliding a knife lengthwise down one of the spines to create an opening, use either your thumb or a spoon to remove the peel from the unripe banana. Slice each banana into 1-inch sections. Place them into the slow cooker and cook on low for another hour.

Bananas should be tender but still firm.

**Step 3**

Allow to cool enough to handle and pour into a large container. Add avocados and carefully mix together. Refrigerate for at least 4 hours before serving.

# Black Beans and White Rice

**MAKES: 4 to 6 servings | PREP TIME: 10 minutes | COOK TIME: 8 hours**

**Ingredients**

- 2 cups dried black beans
- ¾ cup sofrito
- ½ cup chopped canned tomato
- ¾ teaspoon cumin
- ½ teaspoon oregano
- ½ Spanish onion, diced
- 2 garlic cloves, minced
- 4 cups water
- Salt
- Pepper
- ½ cup chopped cilantro

**Directions**

**Step 1**

Rinse and remove any debris from black beans. Add sofrito, tomatoes, cumin, oregano, onions, and garlic to your slow cooker along with 4 cups of water. Stir.

**Step 2**

Set the cooker to low and cook for 8 hours. The beans should be soft but still firm enough to hold their shape. Turn the heat off, add salt and pepper to taste, and stir in the cilantro. Serve over freshly cooked white rice.

# Beef Stew

**MAKES: 8 servings | PREP TIME: 15 minutes | COOK TIME: 25 minutes**

**Ingredients**

- 3 pounds cubed beef
- 2 tablespoons adobo
- 1 teaspoon cumin
- 1 tablespoon flour
- 4 garlic cloves, diced
- 4 tablespoons sofrito

- 1 cup chopped cilantro
- 1 (8-ounce) can tomato sauce
- 1½ teaspoon sazón
- ¼ cup alcaparrado
- 3 peeled potatoes, cut into 1-inch cubes

**Directions**

**Step 1**

Place cubed beef in a large bowl and sprinkle with adobo, cumin, and flour, and toss to coat. Select sauté on the pressure cooker, and add in the seasoned beef in batches, browning on all sides, about 5 minutes per batch.

**Step 2**

Add garlic, sofrito, cilantro, tomato sauce, sazón, and alcaparrado to the pressure cooker. Stir everything together and lock the lid into place. Cook on high pressure for 10 minutes. Let the pressure release naturally for about 5 minutes, then do a quick release.

**Step 3**

Add in the cubed potatoes and replace the lid. Set to high pressure and cook for 2 more minutes. Allow the pressure to release naturally.

VARIATION TIP: You can also make this the traditional stove top way. Sear the meat over medium to high heat in a large pot or caldero, then remove the meat and add in sofrito, cilantro, and garlic, and cook for 2 to 3 minutes. Add in seasonings and enough water to cover meat, then cover and simmer for 30 minutes. Add in potatoes and cook, covered, for another 20 minutes.

# White Bean Soup

**MAKES: 6 servings | PREP TIME: 10 minutes | COOK TIME: 50 minutes**

**Ingredients**

- ½ pound chopped bacon
- ½ pound dry white navy beans
- 1 garlic clove, minced
- ¼ cup sofrito
- ½ cup alcaparrado
- 1 cup tomato sauce
- 8 cups chicken broth
- 2 potatoes, peeled and cubed

**Directions**

**Step 1**

Cook bacon until desired doneness, then remove from pan and set aside.

**Step 2**

Rinse beans thoroughly, then place beans, garlic, sofrito, alcaparrado, tomato sauce, and chicken broth into the pressure cooker. Set the cooker to high pressure for 35 minutes, with a complete natural release.

**Step 3**

After 35 minutes stir in the potatoes, replace the lid, and set to high pressure; cook for another 3 minutes, then do a five-minute natural release followed by a quick release.

VARIATION TIP: If cooking on the stove top, sauté bacon in a large pot until crispy. Remove from the pot and add in sofrito, garlic, and alcaparrado. Cook 2 to 3 minutes until the garlic becomes fragrant. Add in the remainder of the ingredients and stir. Bring to a simmer, cover, and cook for about 20 minutes, then serve.

# Chicken Soup

**MAKES: 6 servings | PREP TIME: 15 minutes | COOK TIME: 10 minutes**

**Ingredients**

- 8 to 10 cups salted water
- 1½ cups angel hair pasta
- 2 tablespoons olive oil
- 2 chicken breasts
- 3 chicken thighs
- 4 garlic cloves, minced
- 2 potatoes, cubed
- 3 carrots, chopped
- 1 bunch of cilantro, chopped
- ½ cup sofrito
- ½ cup alcaparrado
- 2 tablespoons chicken bouillon
- 1½ teaspoon sazón

**Directions**

**Step 1**

Bring about 3 cups of salted water (use no more than ½ teaspoon salt) to a boil. Add in noodles and cook for about 12 minutes. Drain and set aside.

**Step 2**

Drizzle 2 tablespoons of olive oil into the pressure cooker and set to sauté. While oil is heating, cut chicken into about 1-inch bite-size cubes. Brown the chicken in the oil; don't cook it all the way through, just enough to give it a nice sear.

**Step 3**

Add the garlic, potatoes, carrots, cilantro, sofrito, alcaparrado, chicken bouillon, and sazón into the pressure cooker with the chicken. Lock lid into place, set to high pressure, and cook for 4 minutes. When finished, let the pressure release naturally for 5 minutes, then finish with a quick release. When the valve drops remove the lid and stir in the pre-cooked noodles, then serve.

COOKING TIP: I like to cook the noodles separately because I think they become too soft when preparing them in the pressure cooker. You can add in the noodles with the rest of the ingredients if you like them softer.

VARIATION TIP: You can add rice to the recipe to create a heartier meal. With about 2 hours left on the cook time, pour in 1½ cups rice, re-cover, and allow to finish cooking for another 2 hours.

# Chicken Stew

**MAKES: 6 servings | PREP TIME: 15 minutes | COOK TIME: 4 to 8 hours**

**Ingredients**

- 3 chicken breasts, cubed
- 2 potatoes, cubed
- ½ cup alcaparrado
- 3 carrots, chopped
- 1½ teaspoons sazón
- 1 teaspoon adobo
- ½ teaspoon cumin
- ½ teaspoon oregano
- 1 (8-ounce) can tomato sauce
- Water

Put the chicken, potatoes, alcaparrado, carrots, sazón, adobe, cumin, oregano, and tomato sauce into the slow cooker with enough water to submerge everything, and stir. Set to low and cook for 8 hours, set to high for 4 hours. Serve with rice or by itself.

# Puerto Rican Stew

**MAKES: 10 servings | PREP TIME: 20 minutes | COOK TIME: 8 hours**

**Ingredients**

- 1½ pounds top round beef
- 1 yuca, peeled and chopped
- 3 potatoes, peeled and chopped
- 1 yellow plantain, sliced
- 2 green plantains, sliced
- 2 ears corn
- 5 garlic cloves, minced
- ⅓ cup chopped Spanish onions

- ⅓ cup chopped green pepper
- ½ cup chopped cilantro
- 1 tablespoon adobo
- ½ cup sofrito
- 4 quarts (16 cups) beef broth
- Salt
- Pepper

**Directions**

**Step 1**

Chop beef, yuca, and potatoes into roughly 1-inch cubes. Slice the plantains into about 1-inch pieces and the ears of corn into 2-inch pieces.

**Step 2**

Add the beef, yuca, potatoes, plantains, corn, garlic, onions, peppers, cilantro, adobo, sofrito, and beef broth to the slow cooker and stir to combine, adding salt and pepper to taste. Set on low and cook for 6 to 8 hours, until all the starches are tender, then serve.

VARIATION TIP: To make this on the stove top, heat a couple of tablespoons of oil in a caldero or dutch oven. Sauté the garlic and onions until the garlic becomes fragrant. Add cubed beef and brown on all sides. Then add green peppers, cilantro, sofrito, seasonings, and 4 cups of the beef broth. Bring to a boil, then reduce heat and simmer for 20 minutes. Add the rest of the ingredients and beef broth and cook until all the starches are tender.

# Meatballs

**MAKES: 5 servings | PREP TIME: 10 minutes | COOK TIME: 6 to 8 hours**

These cool little meatballs are simple to make but versatile. Serve them over some rice and you have a great dinner, or throw them on a toasted roll and you have the perfect meatball sandwich for lunch. My little brother usually just toasts a little Italian bread to eat with them. He loves using the bread to sop up the sauce, not letting any of it go to waste.

FOR THE MEATBALLS

- 1 pound ground beef
- ½ cup bread crumbs
- ½ cup sofrito
- 1 beaten egg
- ½ bunch cilantro, chopped
- 1 tablespoon oil

FOR THE SAUCE

- 4 cups beef broth
- 1 tablespoon sofrito
- 1 (8-ounce) can tomato sauce

- ¼ cup alcaparrado

TO MAKE THE MEATBALLS

1 . Combine the ground beef, bread crumbs, sofrito, egg, and cilantro in a medium bowl. Form the mixture into roughly 1½-inch balls.

**Step 2**

On the stove top heat 1 tablespoon oil in a sauté pan or skillet over medium to high heat. Sear the meatballs on all sides, 2 to 3 minutes per side. Remove the meatballs and set them aside.

TO MAKE THE SAUCE

Add the beef broth, sofrito, tomato sauce, and alcaparrado into the slow cooker and mix. Add meatballs to the sauce, set to low heat, and cook for 6 to 8 hours.

VARIATION TIP: To make these on the stove top combine all the sauce ingredients in a caldero or dutch oven, then make the meatball mixture. Place the formed meatballs into the sauce and bring to a simmer. Cover and cook for 25 to 30 minutes.

# Steak and Onions

**MAKES: 6 servings | PREP TIME: 5 minutes | COOK TIME: 8 hours**

***Ingredients***

- 2 pounds flank steak
- Salt
- Pepper
- 2 Spanish onions, sliced
- 2 garlic cloves, minced
- ¼ cup red wine vinegar
- 1 cup beef broth
- 2 teaspoons oregano
- 1 tablespoon cumin

**Directions**

**Step 1**

Slice steak into long thin strips and place into the slow cooker. Season with salt and pepper to taste. Cover the steak with the sliced onion and minced garlic.

**Step 2**

In a small bowl mix together the vinegar, beef broth, oregano, and cumin and pour over steak and onions. Set slow cooker to low and cook for 8 hours.

VARIATION TIP: To make this on the stove top, mix together red wine vinegar, ½ cup beef broth, oregano, cumin, and garlic. Place the steak in the marinade, making sure it is completely coated. Cover and place in the refrigerator for at least 8 hours. After marinating, heat 2 tablespoons of oil in a skillet and sauté onions for 3 to 4 minutes. Pour in the other ½ cup of beef broth and let the onions cook, absorbing the broth for another 7 to 10 minutes. Remove the onions from the pan, and in the same pan cook the steak to your preferred temperature.

# Pork Shoulder

**MAKES: 8 to 10 servings | PREP TIME: 4 to 8 hours | COOK TIME: 8 hours**

**Ingredients**

- 6 pounds pork shoulder
- 2 heads garlic
- ½ cup olive oil
- ¼ cup white vinegar
- 2 teaspoons sazón
- 1 teaspoon adobo
- 1 teaspoon oregano
- Pepper

**Directions**

**Step 1**

Make slits in all sides of the pork shoulder. Peel 1 head of garlic and stuff the cloves into the slits you just made.

**Step 2**

Put the olive oil, vinegar, sazón, adobo, oregano, and pepper in a food processor and blend until smooth. Coat the pork shoulder with this mixture, then wrap in plastic wrap and rest in the refrigerator at least overnight.

**Step 3**

Remove the pork from its wrapping and place in the slow cooker on low for 8 hours. Slice, then serve.

VARIATION TIP: Traditionally (the way my dad taught me), pernil is roasted in the oven to give it a crispy skin. To cook it this way, once the pork is done marinating, preheat your oven to 325° F. Once the oven has reached temperature place the pork shoulder in a deep baking dish with at least 2-inch-high sides. Roast for 3½ hours, then turn the heat up to 450° F. Pour about ¼ to ½ cup water into the pan and cook another 35 minutes or until the skin is as crispy as you like it.

INGREDIENT TIP: Choose a nice marbled pork shoulder with plenty of fat as this will help keep it moist during cooking.

# Puerto Rican Sofrito

**MAKES: 4 cups | PREP TIME: 15 minutes**

**Ingredients**

- 1 bunch cilantro
- 1 red bell pepper
- 2 Spanish onions

- 2 green bell peppers
- 4 cubanelle peppers
- 4 culantro leaves
- 10 ajíes dulces (sweet peppers)
- 15 garlic cloves
- 1 tablespoon capers
- **Directions**
- **Step 1**

Wash, peel, seed, and roughly chop the cilantro, bell pepper, Spanish onions, green bell peppers, cubanelle peppers, culantro leaves, ajies dulces, garlic cloves, and capers. Place the onions and cubanelle peppers in a food processor and pulse until finely chopped. Add the cilantro, red bell peppers, green bell peppers, culantro leaves, ajíes dulces, garlic, and capers in and continue blending until smooth.

SUBSTITUTION TIP: There are a couple of ingredients you may have trouble finding, but that's okay; there are simple substitutions. Cubanelle peppers can be replaced with green bell peppers, for a total of 6. If you can't find culantro, add in a little extra cilantro. Ajíes dulces can be replaced with Italian sweet peppers.

STORAGE TIP: I always make plenty of sofrito at a time so I have some on hand whenever I need it. I pour the extra Sofrito into an ice cube tray and freeze it, and I take the cubes and toss them right into whatever I'm making (each cube in my tray is about 2 tablespoons, but yours may be different).

# Achiote Oil

**MAKES: 1 cup | COOK TIME: 15 minutes**

**Ingredients**

- 1 cup olive oil
- 4 tablespoons annatto seeds

**Directions**

**Step 1**

Pour oil and seeds into a saucepan. Bring the oil to a slight simmer over medium heat, then turn the heat down to low and simmer for 2 to 3 minutes. Once the oil has taken on a deep red color, remove from heat.

**Step 2**

Let oil cool to room temperature, then strain the seeds and discard.

STORAGE TIP: Store oil in a sealed jar at room temperature. Achiote will last for 2 to 3 months when properly stored.

# Fried Pork Rinds/Crackling

**MAKES: 10 servings | PREP TIME: 35 minutes | COOK TIME: 3 hours 30 minutes**

**Ingredients**

- 3 pounds pork back fat with skin
- 2 cups oil
- Salt
- Pepper

**Directions**

**Step 1**

Preheat oven to 250°F. Cut the pork into roughly 2-inch-wide strips, then slice along the strip between the skin and the fat, removing the fat from the skin. Cut the strips into 2-by-2-inch cubes.

**Step 2**

Place a wire rack on top of a baking sheet, lay the cubes fat side down on the wire rack. Bake for about 3 hours until the pork skin is completely dried out.

**Step 3**

Heat about 1 inch of oil over medium heat in a pan or skillet on the stove top. Do not allow the oil to start bubbling, place the dried pork skin in oil in batches. Fry for 4 to 5 minutes, until the pork skin bubbles and starts to puff up.

**Step 4**

Remove from oil and place on paper towels to drain excess oil. Salt and pepper pork rinds to taste.

SUBSTITUTION TIP: If you're short on time, chicharrónes can be substituted with store-bought pork rinds, but let's be honest, once you make them from scratch you will never buy them bagged again.

STORAGE TIP: These will keep in the refrigerator for 3 to 4 days.

# Fried Pork Belly

**MAKES: 10 servings | PREP TIME: 1 hour | COOK TIME: 25 minutes**

**Ingredients**

- 2 pounds pork belly
- 1½ tablespoons garlic powder
- 1½ teaspoons sazón
- 1 teaspoon oregano
- Salt
- Pepper
- 2 cups oil

**Directions**

**Step 1**

Cut pork belly into 2-by-2-inch cubes and place in a large bowl. Add the garlic powder, sazón, oregano, salt, and pepper over the pork and toss to coat.

**Step 2**

Heat about 1 inch of oil in a pan or skillet over medium to high heat. Fry seasoned pork chunks until they are a deep brown on all sides, about 10 minutes. Remove pork from the pan and place on paper towels to drain excess oil. Season with salt and pepper to taste and serve immediately.

# Puerto Rican Seasoned Salt

**MAKES: 2 cups | PREP TIME: 5 minutes**

**Ingredients**

- ⅓ cup oregano
- ½ cup garlic powder
- 4 tablespoons onion powder
- 4 tablespoons black pepper
- 4 tablespoons ground cumin
- 4 tablespoons paprika
- 4 tablespoons ground coriander
- 2 tablespoons turmeric

Whisk together the oregano, garlic powder, onion powder, black pepper, ground cumin, paprika, coriander, and turmeric in a medium-size bowl.

STORAGE TIP: Store in a mason jar in a cool, dry place until ready to use. Adobo will last for well over a year.

# Sazón

**MAKES: ⅓ cup | PREP TIME: 5 minutes**

***Ingredients***

- 1 tablespoon ground annatto seeds
- 1 tablespoon ground coriander
- 1 tablespoon cumin
- 1 tablespoon garlic powder
- 1 tablespoon salt
- 2 teaspoons oregano

Whisk together ground annatto seeds, coriander, cumin, garlic powder, salt, and oregano in a medium-size bowl.

STORAGE TIP: Store in a mason jar in a cool, dry place until ready to use. Like most dried seasonings, sazón will last for well over a year.

# Garlic Marinade

**MAKES: 2½ cups | PREP TIME: 15 minutes | COOK TIME: 10 minutes**

***Ingredients***

- ½ cup olive oil
- 10 smashed and peeled garlic cloves
- 1½ cups orange juice
- ½ cup lime juice
- ½ cup lemon juice
- 2 jalapeños, sliced
- Salt

**Directions**

**Step 1**

Heat the oil in a saute pan or skillet over medium heat. Add the garlic and sauté for 1 to 2 minutes until the garlic becomes fragrant.

**Step 2**

Add the orange juice, lime juice, lemon juice, jalapeños, and salt, and cook for 2 to 3 minutes, then remove from heat.

VARIATION TIP: If you prefer a smoother texture, simply pulse in a blender or food processor until smooth.

STORAGE TIP: Mojo Criollo will keep in the refrigerator, covered, for 3 to 4 days.

# Beef Hash

**MAKES: 5 servings | PREP TIME: 5 minutes | COOK TIME: 30 minutes**

**Ingredients**

- 2 tablespoons achiote oil
- ¼ cup sofrito
- ¼ cup alcaparrado
- 1 pound ground beef
- 2 tablespoons tomato paste
- Salt
- Pepper

**Directions**

**Step 1**

Heat achiote oil in a large saute pan or skillet over medium heat. Add in sofrito and alcaparrado and cook for about 5 minutes; the sofrito should be simmering and the moisture just starting to evaporate.

**Step 2**

Add ground beef, breaking it up in the pan, and brown it until most of the moisture evaporates. Stir in tomato paste and cook for 2 to 3 minutes. Remove from heat and add salt and pepper to taste.

VARIATION TIP: Make this recipe your own by adding any of the following before the ground beef is added: ½ cup diced onions, ½ cup diced green peppers, ½ cup chopped cilantro, or 2 chopped culantro leaves.

STORAGE TIP: Picadillo will keep in the refrigerator for 3 to 4 days.

# Olives and Capers

**MAKES: 2 cups | PREP TIME: 15 minutes**

**Ingredients**

- 6 ounces pimento-stuffed green olives
- 3 ounces capers
- ½ cup red wine vinegar
- 2 tablespoons olive oil
- Pepper

Roughly chop green olives and place in a mason jar. Add the capers, vinegar, olive oil, and pepper to the jar and shake well. Store in the refrigerator to allow the flavors to mingle.

STORAGE TIP: Sealed and refrigerated, alcaparrado will last for about 6 weeks.

# Hot Pepper and Garlic Sauce

**MAKES: 2 cups | PREP TIME: 15 minutes**

**Ingredients**

- 6 jalapeños, seeded and chopped
- 8 to 10 garlic cloves, minced
- 6 peppercorns
- ¼ cup lime juice
- ½ cup olive oil
- 2 teaspoons salt

Put the jalapenos, garlic cloves, peppercorns, lime juice, olive oil, and salt into a food processor and blend until smooth. Seal in a jar and refrigerate.

STORAGE TIP: Ajili Mojili will keep in the refrigerator for 3 to 4 days.

# Puerto Rican Hot Sauce

**MAKES: 2 cups | PREP TIME: 15 minutes plus 2 days resting**

**Ingredients**

- 5 habanero peppers
- 5 jalapeño peppers
- 1 Spanish onion, sliced

- 10 garlic cloves, halved and mashed
- 10 peppercorns
- ⅓ teaspoon salt
- 1 cup apple cider vinegar (extra if needed to fill your jar)

**Directions**

**Step 1**

Remove the stems from the habanero peppers and jalapeno peppers and quarter them lengthwise (do not remove the seeds).

**Step 2**

Place peppers in a large jar and add onions, garlic, peppercorns, and salt. Fill the rest of the jar with apple cider vinegar leaving about ½ inch of space between the vinegar and the top of the jar. Close the jar tightly and shake to combine all the ingredients. Allow to sit for at least 2 days at room temperature.

STORAGE TIP: Pique will keep for a couple of months when refrigerated in a sealed container.

SUBSTITUTION TIP: Traditionally this is made with ají caballeros, but I know those can be difficult to find. In their place, you can use habaneros.

VARIATION TIP: I use a 50/50 split of habaneros and jalapeños. You can increase the heat by using more habaneros than jalapeños, or decrease the heat by using more jalapeños than habaneros.

# Garlic Dipping Sauce

**MAKES: 2½ cups | PREP TIME: 15 minutes**

**Ingredients**

- 1 cup olive oil
- 8 to 10 garlic cloves, minced
- 1 Spanish onion, chopped
- 3 tablespoons chopped cilantro
- 2 tablespoons lemon juice
- 2 tablespoons lime juice
- Salt

Put the olive oil, garlic cloves, onion, cilantro, lemon juice, lime juice, and salt in a food processor and blend until smooth. Seal in a jar and refrigerate.

STORAGE TIP: Mojito will keep in the refrigerator for 3 to 4 days.

INGREDIENT TIP: This garlic dipping sauce is not to be confused with Mojo de Ajo/Garlic Sauce. To make Mojo de Ajo, place 1 cup of oil and 10 peeled and crushed garlic cloves in a small saucepan and simmer for about 20 minutes. Once cool, blend in a food processor until smooth.

# Pink Sauce

**MAKES: 1½ cups | PREP TIME: 10 minutes**

***Ingredients***

- 1 cup mayonnaise
- 6 tablespoons ketchup
- 1 garlic clove, minced

In a small bowl, whisk the mayonnaise, ketchup, and garlic clove together. Place in a mason jar, seal, and refrigerate until you are ready to use.

VARIATION TIP: Add in hot sauce or a little salt and pepper to taste until you get the flavor or heat you want.

STORAGE TIP: Salsa Rosa will keep in the refrigerator, covered, for 3 to 4 days.

# Island Sauce Dip

**MAKES: 3½ cups | PREP TIME: 5 minutes**

**Ingredients**

- ¼ cup olive oil
- 1 Spanish onion, chopped
- 1 green pepper, chopped
- 4 garlic cloves, minced
- ½ cup alcaparrado
- 1 cup tomato sauce
- 1 bunch cilantro
- Salt
- Pepper

**Directions**

**Step 1**

In a saute pan or skillet, heat the oil over medium heat. Sauté the onions and bell peppers until onions start to become translucent.

**Step 2**

Add garlic, and cook until the garlic becomes fragrant. Add in the alcaparrado, tomato sauce, cilantro, salt, and pepper and cook for another 10 minutes.

VARIATION TIP: If you want a little heat in your Mojito Isleño, go ahead and add some pique to your taste.

STORAGE TIP: Mojito Isleño will keep in the refrigerator, covered, for 3 to 4 days.

# Chimichurri

**MAKES: 1 cup | PREP TIME: 5 minutes**

**Ingredients**

- ½ cup finely chopped cilantro
- ½ cup finely chopped parsley
- 2 tablespoons oregano
- 3 tablespoons minced red onion
- 1 tablespoon minced garlic
- ⅛ teaspoon adobo
- Olive oil

In a small bowl, mix the cilantro, parsley, oregano, onions, garlic, and adobo, then drizzle in a little olive oil, stirring until completely combined.

STORAGE TIP: Chimichurri will keep for about 3 days when covered and refrigerated.

# Preparing Plantain/Banana Leaves

**MAKES: 10 to 20 leaves | PREP TIME: 5 minutes | COOK TIME: 10 minutes**

**Ingredients**

- 10 to 20 plantain/ banana leaves

**Directions**

**Step 1**

Preheat oven to 200°F. Cut the leaves to the size you need; this will vary depending on the recipe. Pasteles will need a larger-size leaf, while Guanimes need a much smaller-size leaf.

**Step 2**

Place leaves on a baking sheet in a single layer, careful not to overlap them. Bake for 5 to 10 minutes, until the leaves are soft and pliable. Use immediately after preparing.

COOKING TIP: You can prep the leaves on the stove top by turning on one of the burners and slowly passing the leaf about 1 to 1½ inches above the flame. The leaves will darken to a deep green, but you don't want to burn them. Heat them just enough to make them pliable.

INGREDIENT TIP: If you want to give any of the dishes in this book a real island look and feel, line your serving plates with banana leaves; simply cut the leaf to the size of your plate before you serve your dish.

# Piña Colada

**MAKES: 4 drinks | PREP TIME: 5 minutes**

**Ingredients**

- 3 cups ice
- 12 ounces pineapple juice
- 6 ounces light rum
- 4 ounces coconut cream
- 2 ounces dark rum

**Directions**

**Step 1**

Place ice, pineapple juice, light rum, coconut cream, and dark rum into a blender. Blend until completely smooth.

**Step 2**

Pour into 4 glasses and serve immediately.

**SERVING TIP:** Serve in hollowed-out coconuts with a slice of pineapple on the rim of each to feel like you're on the island, wherever you are.

**ENTERTAINING TIP:** This recipe is a simple 1 part coconut cream, 2 parts rum, and 3 parts juice. If you're entertaining for a crowd, simply scale up as necessary.

# Puerto Rican Eggnog

**MAKES: 10 drinks | PREP TIME: 1 hour (plus 2 to 3 hours chill time)**

**Ingredients**

- 1 cup dark rum
- 2 cinnamon sticks
- 2 (13.5-ounce) cans coconut milk
- 1 (14-ounce) can condensed milk
- ½ teaspoon vanilla extract
- ½ teaspoon ground cinnamon

**Directions**

**Step 1**

In a jar with a lid add rum and cinnamon sticks. Close and allow to sit for 1 hour.

**Step 2**

In a blender, add the coconut milk, condensed milk, vanilla extract, and ground cinnamon and purée. Pour in rum and cinnamon stick mixture and shake well to make sure they are combined.

**Step 3**

Pour everything into a large bottle or pitcher and refrigerate at least 2 to 3 hours. The drink will thicken the longer it rests.

VARIATION TIP: If you like a thinner drink add in about ½ cup water to the ingredients.

STORAGE TIP: The longer coquito rests, the stronger the flavor gets. You can allow it to rest for up to a month in the refrigerator before serving.

# Limón Cocktail

**MAKES: 4 drinks | PREP TIME: 5 minutes**

**Ingredients**

- 4 ounces Bacardí Limón
- 4 ounces coconut rum

- 4 ounces pineapple juice
- Ice
- 4 lime wedges, for garnish
- **Directions**
- **Step 1**
- Combine Bacardi Limón, coconut rum, and pineapple juice in a shaker with ice. Shake well and strain into chilled cocktail glasses. Garnish with a slice of lime and serve.

MAKE-AHEAD TIP: You can make this ahead of time and allow it to chill in a pitcher in the refrigerator.

# Cuba Libre

**MAKES: 1 drink | PREP TIME: 3 minutes**

**Ingredients**

- ½ lime
- Ice cubes
- 2 ounces light rum
- 4 ounces cola
- **Directions**
- **Step 1**

Squeeze juice from the lime into a tall glass and add in ice cubes. Pour in the rum and cola, stir well, and enjoy.

**ENTERTAINING TIP:** This recipe is a simple 2 parts cola, 1 part rum, and the juice of half a lime per glass. Simply scale up that ratio if you're serving a crowd.

INGREDIENT TIP: After juicing the lime, muddle it in the glass, then remove it. Muddled lime makes this drink really pop.

# Daiquiri

**MAKES: 1 drink | PREP TIME: 5 minutes**

- 2 ounces light rum
- 1 ounce fresh lime juice, plus 1 lime wedge
- 1 ounce simple syrup
- Ice
- **Directions**
- **Step 1**

Nothing says tropical paradise like a nice chilled drink, and nothing says chilled drink like a daiquiri. This classic cocktail is refreshing, light, and easy to make. Everything you need can be found in any major grocery store. This daquiri is a sweeter drink thanks to the simple syrup, and it goes down easy. Kick back and enjoy.

**Step 2**

Combine rum, lime juice, and simple syrup in a shaker with ice. Shake well and strain into a chilled cocktail glass. Garnish with a slice of lime and serve.

**ENTERTAINING TIP:** This recipe is a simple 2 parts rum, 1 part lime juice, and 1 part simple syrup. Scale up as necessary for entertaining a crowd.

# Mojito

**MAKES: 1 drink | PREP TIME: 5 minutes**

**Ingredients**

- 12 fresh mint leaves
- ½ lime cut into 4 slices
- 2 tablespoons granulated sugar
- 1 cup ice
- 1½ ounces light rum
- ½ cup club soda

**Directions**

**Step 1**

Muddle the mint and 1 slice of lime in a glass. Add sugar and 2 more slices of lime and muddle again. (If you don't have a muddler, use the handle of a wooden spoon to crush the ingredients.)

**Step 2**

Add in ice, and pour rum and club soda over the ice. Stir and serve.

**ENTERTAINING TIP:** Making a pitcher is very simple. Quadruple the amounts of all the ingredients and add to a pitcher. Refrigerate until you are ready to use.

# Yellow Bird Cocktail

**MAKES: 1 drink | PREP TIME: 5 minutes**

**Ingredients**

- ½ lime
- Ice
- 1¼ ounces orange juice
- 1 ounce light rum
- 1 ounce dark rum
- ¼ ounce Galliano liqueur

**Directions**

**Step 1**

Juice the lime into a shaker with ice and add the orange juice, light and dark rums, and the Galliano liqueur.

**Step 2**

Shake well and strain into a tall glass filled with ice.

VARIATION TIP: Pour 1½ ounces each of light and dark rum into a glass, then add 2 ounces each of a banana liqueur and orange juice.

# Guava Margarita

**MAKES: 4 drinks | PREP TIME: 15 minutes**

**Ingredients**

- ½ cup fresh lime juice
- 1 cup tequila
- ½ cup Grand Marnier
- 1 cup guava purée
- Coarse salt

**Directions**

**Step 1**

Mix together lime juice, tequila, Grand Marnier, and guava purée in a large pitcher. Refrigerate until ready to use.

**Step 2**

To serve, rub a cut lime around the rim of each serving glass, and press the rim into salt. Pour margarita into salt-prepped glass.

# Coconut Milk

**MAKES: 2 to 3 cups | PREP TIME: 40 minutes**

**Ingredients**

- 1 large coconut
- 2 to 3 cups water

**Directions**

**Step 1**

Using a screwdriver, pierce one of the eyes in the coconut and tap the end of the screwdriver with a hammer or mallet. Drain the liquid (you can drink it or store it in the refrigerator for up to 4 days).

**Step 2**

Crack open the coconut using a hammer and break it into small pieces. Carefully run a knife between the shell and the white part of the coconut to remove the meat. If small bits of shell remain on the meat you can use a vegetable peeler to remove them.

**Step 3**

Place the coconut meat into a blender and pour in water. Make sure there is enough water to cover all the coconut meat. Blend until it is finely grated.

**Step 4**

Place cheesecloth into a sieve, and place over the container of your choice. Pour the coconut mixture into the cheesecloth and squeeze as much liquid as possible into the container.

5 . Refrigerate coconut milk and serve within 3 to 4 days.

INGREDIENT TIP: Bake your coconut for 30 minutes at 350°F. This will coconut meat and make it easier to remove once it has cooled. You can also purchase packaged coconut at many stores and online; simply chop it into small pieces and add it to the blender.

# Rice Milk

**MAKES: 4 cups | PREP TIME: 1 day**

**Ingredients**

- 1 cup white rice
- 5½ cups water, divided
- 1 teaspoon honey
- ¼ teaspoon vanilla extract

**Directions**

**Step 1**

Place rinsed rice into a bowl and cover with 1½ cups of water. Allow to soak overnight.

**Step 2**

Drain the water from rice. Put the rice and the remaining 4 cups of water into a blender and pulse for 1 to 2 minutes. Place a sieve lined with cheesecloth over a bowl and strain the mixture through the cloth. Squeeze the cloth to get as much liquid out as possible.

**Step 3**

Mix honey and vanilla extract into milk and place into mason jars or a pitcher, allowing it to chill until ready to serve.

STORAGE TIP: Rice milk will keep in the refrigerator for up to 1 week.

# Star Fruit Juice

**MAKES: 8 cups | PREP TIME: 15 minutes**

**Ingredients**

- 10 star fruits
- 4 cups water
- ½ cup granulated sugar
- Ice

**Directions**

**Step 1**

Halve each star fruit and squeeze the ends to push the pulp out of the skin. Place the pulps into a blender.

**Step 2**

Add the water and sugar and pulse until liquified. Pour through a strainer into a pitcher with ice.

INGREDIENT TIP: A ripe, flavorful star fruit will be yellow to yellow-green in color. If it's more green than yellow, it's not ready to be used yet.

# Guava Smoothie

**MAKES: 4 drinks | PREP TIME: 10 minutes**

**Ingredients**

- 1 (14-ounce) package guava pulp
- 1 (12-ounce) can evaporated milk
- 1 cup water
- ½ cup granulated sugar
- 1 teaspoon vanilla extract
- Ice
- **Directions**
- **Step 1**

Place guava pulp, evaporated milk, water, sugar, and vanilla extract in a blender and pulse until liquified. To serve, fill glasses with ice and pour smoothie over ice.

# Guava Dip

**MAKES: 2 cups | PREP TIME: 15 minutes**

**Ingredients**

- 5 ounces guava paste
- 2 tablespoons water
- 8 ounces softened cream cheese
- ¼ cup sour cream
- 2 tablespoons honey
- 1 minced garlic clove
- Salt

**Directions**

**Step 1**

Place guava paste and water into a food processor and pulse until smooth. Remove paste and set aside. Rinse out processor.

**Step 2**

Place the cream cheese, sour cream, honey, garlic, and salt into the food processor and pulse until smooth. Transfer to a serving bowl and fold the guava paste into the cheese mixture.

STORAGE TIP: Tightly cover the dip and store it in the refrigerator for up to 1 week.

# Puerto Rican Oatmeal

**MAKES: 2 servings | COOK TIME: 25 minutes**

**Ingredients**

- 1¾ cups condensed milk
- Salt
- Sugar
- 1 tablespoon butter
- 1 small cinnamon stick
- 1 cup oats
- Ground cinnamon, for garnish

**Directions**

**Step 1**

In a medium saucepan, bring condensed milk to a simmer. Add in the salt, sugar, butter, and cinnamon stick. Bring to a full boil, making sure everything except the cinnamon stick is completely combined.

**Step 2**

Add in oats and turn the heat down, stirring occasionally until oats are cooked to your desired consistency.

**Step 3**

Remove from the heat and discard the cinnamon stick. Cover the saucepan and allow to rest for 2 to 3 minutes. Garnish with cinnamon before serving.

COOKING TIP: You can make Avena in the microwave by putting all the ingredients in a large microwave-safe bowl and heating at 50 percent power for 5 to 8 minutes.

SUBSTITUTION TIP: You can use regular whole milk in place of condensed milk.

# Shrimp Salad

**MAKES: 6 servings | PREP TIME: 10 minutes | COOK TIME: 5 minutes**

**Ingredients**

- 3 tablespoons butter
- 3 pounds shrimp, deveined and tails removed
- ¼ cup chopped green pepper
- ¼ cup chopped red pepper
- ¼ cup chopped red onion
- ¼ cup olives
- ½ lemon, juiced
- Salt

- Pepper

**Directions**

**Step 1**

Melt butter in a sauté pan or skillet over medium to low heat. Add in shrimp, stirring constantly until shrimp is pink and opaque. Remove shrimp from the pan and allow to cool for several minutes.

**Step 2**

Toss shrimp, green peppers, red peppers, red onions, olives, and lemon juice in a large bowl, making sure everything gets a nice coating of lemon juice. Season with salt and pepper to taste.

SUBSTITUTION TIP: Use frozen or pre-cooked shrimp to save time. If buying shrimp directly from the freezer case, simply thaw in the refrigerator before tossing with other ingredients. If buying frozen, thaw under cold running water, then pat dry.

# Pickled Cassava Salad

**MAKES: 6 servings | PREP TIME: 10 minutes | COOK TIME: 20 minutes**

***Ingredients***

- 1 pound yuca/cassava
- Water
- ⅔ cup olive oil
- 1 white onion, sliced
- 3 garlic cloves, minced
- 3 tablespoons white vinegar
- 7 to 8 pimento-stuffed green olives
- Salt
- Pepper

**Directions**

**Step 1**

Peel the skin from the yuca and chop it into 1-inch chunks.

**Step 2**

Bring a large pot of water to a boil. Add in the chopped yuca and boil for 10 to 15 minutes. Drain and rinse the yuca, and set aside.

**Step 3**

Heat olive oil in a sauté pan or skillet over medium heat. Add in the onions and cook until they soften but before they turn brown, about 5 minutes. Add garlic and vinegar and simmer for another 2 to 3 minutes.

**Step 4**

Toss the yuca, the mixture from step 3, and the green olives together in a large bowl and let rest for at least 1 hour before serving.

COOKING TIP: Make this recipe a day before you eat it and store in the refrigerator. The flavors will mingle and have more of a pop to them when you serve it.

VARIATION TIP: For a punch of extra flavor, add some capers—a popular addition to this recipe.

# Meat Turnovers

**MAKES: 10 pastelillos | PREP TIME: 15 minutes | COOK TIME: 10 minutes**

**Ingredients**

- 3½ cups flour
- 2½ teaspoons salt
- 2 teaspoons baking powder
- 3½ tablespoons vegetable oil
- 1 lightly beaten egg
- ¾ cups cold water
- 1 cup picadillo
- 2 cups oil

**Directions**

**Step 1**

Whisk flour, salt, and baking powder together, combining completely. Slowly whisk in the oil and egg. Add the cold water last and mix until combined.

**Step 2**

Divide dough into 10 equal pieces. Working on a lightly floured surface, roll out dough into roughly 6-inch circles.

**Step 3**

Add about 1 tablespoon of picadillo to each. Using your finger, brush the edge of the dough with water, fold over, and press the edges together with a fork.

**Step 4**

Heat the oil in a sauté pan or skillet over a medium heat (there should be about 2 inches of oil in the pan). When the oil is hot, fry turnovers for 2 to 3 minutes per side, until the dough is golden and flaky. Place turnovers on a paper towel to drain excess oil and cool.

SUBSTITUTION TIP : Goya sells premade dough called discos, which can be used for these turnovers instead of making your own dough.

VARIATION TIP: Picadillo is the traditional filling in these turnovers, but you can use cheese or crab, or any other protein.

# Bean Stew

**MAKES: 6 servings | PREP TIME: 5 minutes | COOK TIME: 25 minutes**

**Ingredients**

- 2 tablespoons sofrito
- 1 tablespoon sazón
- 1 tablespoon adobo
- 1 (8-ounce) can tomato sauce
- ½ cup pimento-stuffed green olives
- 1 teaspoon alcaparrado
- 2 (15-ounce) cans kidney beans
- ½ pound potatoes, cubed
- Water

**Directions**

**Step 1**

Pour in the sofrito, sazón, adobo, and tomato sauce to a large pot over medium heat. Once it starts to sizzle add in olives and alcaparrado. Allow to simmer for 2 to 3 minutes.

**Step 2**

Add the beans, potatoes, and 2 cans' worth of water. Turn heat to high, cover, and boil for 20 minutes. Serve over white rice.

VARIATION TIP: Feel free to use any type of beans in place of kidney beans; this versatile recipe will work well with pinto beans, black beans, and chickpeas.

# Cassava with Garlic Sauce

**MAKES: 4 servings | PREP TIME: 5 minutes | COOK TIME: 25 minutes**

**Ingredients**

- 1½ pounds yuca, peeled and chopped
- Water
- 1 onion, thinly sliced
- ¼ cup orange juice
- ¼ cup lime juice
- 1 tablespoon chopped cilantro
- 4 garlic cloves, minced
- ¼ cup olive oil
- ½ teaspoon oregano
- ½ teaspoon cumin
- Salt
- Pepper

**Directions**

**Step 1**

Place 1-inch yuca chunks into a large pot and cover with water. Bring to a boil and cook for 15 to 20 minutes, until the yuca becomes tender. Drain and set aside in a large bowl.

**Step 2**

In another bowl toss together onions, orange juice, lime juice, cilantro, and garlic. Pour over yuca and set aside.

**Step 3**

Heat oil in a saucepan over medium to high heat and add oregano, cumin, salt, and pepper. Cook until hot and pour over the yuca mixture.

COOKING TIP: You can cook the yuca ahead of time and reheat it in the microwave if you're in a time crunch.

# Garlic Rice with Shrimp

**MAKES: 4 servings | PREP TIME: 5 minutes | COOK TIME: 20 minutes**

**Ingredients**

- ½ pound medium shrimp, peeled and deveined
- 1 teaspoon paprika
- Salt
- Pepper
- ¼ cup chopped bacon
- 4 tablespoons butter
- 5 garlic cloves, minced
- 3 green onions, diced
- 3 cups cooked white rice

**Directions**

**Step 1**

Place shrimp in a medium bowl and add paprika, salt, and pepper to taste. Toss shrimp so it is evenly coated with seasoning.

**Step 2**

Cook chopped bacon in a sauté pan or skillet. Once bacon is cooked to the point you like it, add shrimp and cook until pink and opaque. Remove shrimp and bacon from pan but don't drain the fat.

**Step 3**

Melt butter in the same pan over medium heat, then add garlic and green onion. Once the garlic becomes fragrant add in the cooked rice, stirring so it absorbs the garlic sauce.

**Step 4**

Add shrimp and bacon back in, stir and cook for 1 to 2 minutes, then serve.

# Fried Chicken

**MAKES: 4 servings | PREP TIME: 20 minutes | COOK TIME: 5 minutes**

**Ingredients**

- 2 pounds chicken thighs
- 3 tablespoons olive oil
- 1 tablespoon white vinegar
- 2 garlic cloves, minced
- 1 teaspoon oregano
- Salt
- Pepper
- 1 cup flour
- 2 cups oil

**Directions**

**Step 1**

Rinse and pat chicken dry. Drizzle with olive oil and vinegar, coating chicken on both sides. Add garlic, oregano, salt, and pepper, and rub to make sure chicken is completely coated in seasonings. Cover and set aside for 15 minutes.

**Step 2**

After 15 minutes, toss chicken in flour.

3 . Heat oil in a large pot over high heat. Add flour-coated chicken and fry until golden and crispy, 3 to 5 minutes per side.

COOKING TIP: You can marinate and refrigerate the chicken a day ahead of time. Marinating for a full day will give it great flavor.

# Fried Pork Chunks

**MAKES: 8 servings | PREP TIME: 20 minutes | COOK TIME: 5 minutes**

**Ingredients**

- 2 pounds pork shoulder
- 1 tablespoon sazón
- 1 teaspoon adobo
- 1 teaspoon oregano
- 5 garlic cloves, minced
- 3 tablespoons olive oil
- ⅓ cup vinegar
- 2 cups vegetable or canola oil

**Directions**

**Step 1**

Cut the pork into 1-inch cubes and season with sazón, adobo, oregano, garlic, olive oil, and vinegar, making sure pork is coated evenly. Cover and refrigerate for 20 minutes.

**Step 2**

Heat about 2 cups of oil in a large sauté pan or skillet over medium heat. Add pork to heated oil and fry for about 5 minutes. Remove from oil and place on paper towels to absorb excess oil, then serve.

# Pork Chops

**MAKES: 4 servings | PREP TIME: 5 minutes | COOK TIME: 20 minutes**

**Ingredients**

- 2 tablespoons olive oil, divided
- 2 pounds bone-in pork chops
- 1 tablespoon white vinegar
- 2 teaspoons adobo
- 1 teaspoon sazón
- ½ teaspoon garlic powder

**Directions**

**Step 1**

Drizzle 1 tablespoon olive oil over pork chops and rub to coat. Season with vinegar, adobo, sazón, and garlic powder, making sure the chops are completely coated.

**Step 2**

In a sauté pan or skillet heat the remaining tablespoon of oil over medium to high heat. When hot, sear pork chops about 2 minutes on each side. Once they have a nice sear, reduce the heat and cook another 5 minutes on each side.

COOKING TIP: For a stronger flavor, marinate ahead of time. Mix all seasonings with ½ cup olive oil and coat the chops evenly, then refrigerate for 1 to 2 hours before frying.

# White Rice with Corned Beef

**MAKES: 6 servings | PREP TIME: 5 minutes | COOK TIME: 25 minutes**

**Ingredients**

- 2 cups water
- Pinch salt
- 1 cup uncooked white rice
- 1 teaspoon olive oil
- 2 tablespoons sofrito
- 1 teaspoon oregano
- 1 tablespoon sazón
- Pepper

- 1 (8-ounce) can tomato sauce
- 2 (12-ounce) cans corned beef
- ½ cup corn kernels
- 1 potato, peeled and diced

**Directions**

**Step 1**

In a small saucepan, boil 2 cups of water with a pinch of salt, then add rice. Cover and simmer for 20 minutes.

**Step 2**

While the rice cooks, heat olive oil in a large pan over medium heat. Add sofrito, oregano, sazón, pepper, and tomato sauce, cooking for a couple of minutes.

**Step 3**

Add corned beef. Break apart the beef and cook for a couple of minutes. Mix in the corn kernels and potatoes and cover. Cook for 15 to 20 minutes, stirring occasionally.

**Step 4**

Divide rice among plates and add corned beef on top of the rice.

**SERVING TIP:** The Plátanos Maduros are a perfect side to round out this authentic Puerto Rican dinner.

# Skirt Steak

**MAKES: 4 servings | PREP TIME: 5 minutes | COOK TIME: 12 minutes**

**Ingredients**

- 1½ pounds skirt steak
- ½ teaspoon cumin
- ½ teaspoon ground coriander
- Salt
- Pepper

**Directions**

**Step 1**

Pat the steaks dry. In a small bowl mix cumin, ground coriander, salt, and pepper together and rub the steak with the mixture, coating it evenly.

**Step 2**

Set oven to broil, and broil steak for about 5 minutes per side. Remove steak from the oven and rest for at least 5 minutes.

**Step 3**

Thinly slice steaks holding your knife at a roughly 45-degree angle, then serve.

**SERVING TIP:** Mofongo is the perfect side to have with churrasco. You can also drizzle a little chimichurri over the steak to give it some punch.

# Guava and Cheese Dumplings

**MAKES: 10 dumplings | PREP TIME: 10 minutes | COOK TIME: 10 minutes**

**Ingredients**

- 3½ cups flour
- 2½ teaspoons salt
- 2 teaspoons baking powder
- 3½ tablespoons olive oil
- 1 lightly beaten egg
- ¾ cup cold water
- 10 ounces guava paste
- 8 ounces cream cheese
- Canola or vegetable oil

**Directions**

**Step 1**

Whisk flour, salt, and baking powder together. Once completely combined, slowly whisk in the oil and egg. Add in the cold water last and mix until combined.

**Step 2**

Divide dough into 10 equal pieces. Working on a lightly floured surface, roll out dough into roughly 6-inch circles.

**Step 3**

Cube the guava paste and cream cheese into ¼-inch chunks. Spoon equal amounts of cheese and guava into the center of each dough circle. Brush a little water around the edge of each disk and fold in half, pressing the edges together with a fork.

**Step 4**

Heat about 2 inches of oil in a pan over medium heat. Once the oil begins to simmer fry the pastries until they are golden brown, 2 to 3 minutes per side. Let cool on a paper towel and serve.

# Cornmeal Hot Cereal

**MAKES: 3 to 4 servings | COOK TIME: 20 minutes**

***Ingredients***

- 3 tablespoons butter
- 1½ cups milk
- 1½ cups water
- Pinch sugar
- Pinch salt

- 1½ cups cornmeal

**Directions**

**Step 1**

In a medium saucepan, melt butter and add milk and water. Stir in sugar and salt to taste and bring the mixture to a boil.

**Step 2**

Slowly whisk in cornmeal until combined, 2 to 3 minutes. Continue to cook over a medium heat until the funche thickens, then remove from heat and serve.

VARIATION TIP: Funche is usually served one of two ways. The first is as a hot breakfast cereal with some of your favorite sliced fruit on top, or a splash of cream. The other way is to pour it into a large ramekin or a greased pan, then place it in the refrigerator to cool. Once it is cooled and hardened, turn it over onto a serving dish and slice it.

# Sweet Coconut Cakes

**MAKES: 20 cakes | PREP TIME: 40 minutes | COOK TIME: 10 minutes**

**Ingredients**

- 2 cups flour
- 1 teaspoon baking powder
- 1 cup sugar
- Pinch salt
- 1 cup coconut milk
- ½ cup vegetable oil

**Directions**

**Step 1**

In a medium bowl whisk together flour, baking powder, and sugar until completely combined, and add a pinch of salt to taste. Slowly whisk in coconut milk, stirring until just combined.

**Step 2**

Lightly flour your hands and knead the dough until it's completely incorporated and becomes sticky. Cover the bowl and allow dough to rest for 30 minutes.

**Step 3**

Lightly flour a flat surface to work on. Take half the dough and roll it out until it is about ⅛-inch thick. Using a cookie cutter (a 2-inch one will work), cut out your arepas and set aside. Repeat this process with the second half of the dough. You'll have about 20 arepas in total.

**Step 4**

In a large sauté pan or skillet heat ½ cup vegetable oil. Carefully lower arepas into oil and fry until the edges become a golden color, about 1 minute. Turn arepas and fry another 45 seconds to 1 minute.

5 . Transfer arepas to a paper towel to drain excess oil. Serve while they are warm and crisp.

VARIATION TIP: For an even sweeter taste sprinkle a little bit of cinnamon and sugar over the arepas before serving. For a savory arepa, use whole milk instead of coconut milk and only a pinch of sugar, and add in a teaspoon of garlic powder when mixing the dough.

# Shredded Plantain Fritters

**MAKES: 15 to 20 fritters | PREP TIME: 25 minutes | COOK TIME: 20 minutes**

***Ingredients***

- 3 green plantains
- Garlic salt
- 1 cup oil

**Directions**

**Step 1**

Cut both ends off of the plantains. Find one of the ribs that runs lengthwise and slice along it. Remove the skin using your fingers or a spoon. Halve the peeled plantains and shred with a cheese grater into a large bowl.

**Step 2**

Cover the shredded plantains in water and add garlic salt to taste, soaking for 10 minutes (this will allow them to absorb the garlic flavor). Drain the water and place shredded plantains on a paper towel to absorb excess liquid.

**Step 3**

In a sauté pan or skillet, heat oil over medium to high heat. Scoop 1 heaping tablespoon at a time of the shredded plantains and roll into small balls. Press the balls flat and place them carefully into the heated oil, frying until they are bright yellow, 2 to 3 minutes per side.

4 . Remove the arañitas and place onto a paper towel to drain excess oil, then serve.

# Puerto Rican Fritters

**MAKES: 10 to 15 alcapurrias | PREP TIME: 1 hour 30 minutes | COOK TIME: 10 minutes**

***Ingredients***

- Salted water
- 5 green (unripe) bananas
- 1 pound yautía/taro root
- 1½ tablespoons achiote oil
- Salt
- 1 pound picadillo, fresh (see here ) or canned
- 2 cups oil

**Directions**

**Step 1**

Fill a large bowl with salted water and peel bananas and yautía. Slice the bananas into roughly 1-inch sections. Chop the yautía likewise into about 1-inch cubes. Place bananas and yautía in the salted water and soak for at least 10 to 15 minutes.

**Step 2**

Drain the water, then place the small chunks into a food processor and pulse until they are finely diced. Place the mixture in a large bowl and add 1 tablespoon achiote oil, stirring until mixture takes on the color of the oil evenly. Refrigerate your dough mixture for at least 1 hour, and up to overnight.

**Step 3**

After the dough has rested brush ½ tablespoon of achiote oil on a piece of wax paper. Scoop ¼ cup of the dough onto the wax paper and spread it out into a rough circle with a spoon. Scoop about 1 tablespoon picadillo into the center, then carefully fold the wax paper to bring the edges of the dough together and pinch to seal.

**Step 4**

Heat about 2 cups oil in a large sauté pan or skillet over medium to high heat. Using a spoon, carefully place alcapurrias into the heated oil and fry until golden, 2 to 3 minutes per side. Remove from oil and place on paper towels to drain excess oil. Serve warm, with a side of pique .

VARIATION TIPS: My dad put his own spin on this recipe; instead of achiote oil, he would use about 1 tablespoon of sazón to add coloring to the masa (dough) mixture. While I have only made my alcapurrias with picadillo, my brother makes his with many different fillings, like shrimp or chicken. Get creative with your fillings!

MAKE-AHEAD TIP: You can easily make these a few days ahead of time. Complete steps 1 through 3, then refrigerate for up to 3 days.

# Stuffed Potatoes

**MAKES: 10 servings | PREP TIME: 15 minutes | COOK TIME: 40 minutes**

**Ingredients**

- 2 pounds potatoes
- Water
- Salt
- 4 tablespoons butter
- 1 egg
- ½ cup cornstarch
- 1 pound picadillo, fresh (see here ) or canned
- 2 cups oil

**Directions**

**Step 1**

Peel and cut potatoes into about 1-inch cubes, then place them in a large pot with enough water to cover potatoes. Add a little salt to the water, and boil potatoes about 20 minutes until they are soft and fork tender.

**Step 2**

Drain the water and place potatoes in a large bowl with the butter, egg, salt to taste, and 1 tablespoon cornstarch. Mash ingredients together; they will be a little thicker and dryer than regular mashed potatoes. Let cool enough to be handled with your bare hands.

**Step 3**

Divide the potatoes into 10 equal portions. Lightly coat your hands with flour and roll the potatoes into balls. Create an indent in the center of each and spoon in about 1 tablespoon of picadillo. Close up the potato around the meat and roll the ball in the remaining cornstarch.

**Step 4**

Heat 2 cups of oil in a sauté pan o# skillet over medium heat. Place the balls into the heated oil and fry until golden on all sides, 1 to 2 minutes. Remove from skillet and place on paper towels to drain excess oil and cool.

SUBSTITUTION TIP: You can easily make this recipe with instant mashed potatoes. Follow the instructions on the package and add adobo to taste to season the potatoes. Remember, you want the potatoes to be thick and dry to work with, so use slightly less liquid than what the package instructions call for.

# Cassava Bread

**MAKES: 5 flatbreads | PREP TIME: 15 minutes | COOK TIME: 15 minutes**

***Ingredients***

- 1 pound yuca (cassava root)
- Salt

**Directions**

**Step 1**

Peel and grate the yuca using the finest grate. Place finely grated yuca into a cheesecloth and squeeze excess moisture into a bowl. You want to remove as much liquid as possible.

**Step 2**

Place grated yuca into a bowl and add a pinch of salt. Break apart the yuca, making sure there are no clumps, and divide into 5 equal portions.

**Step 3**

Heat a skillet over low to medium heat. Once the pan is hot, place one portion of grated yuca in the center of the pan, using a spatula to spread it out. Cook until golden, 2 to 3 minutes, then flip and cook the other side until golden. Repeat with the other portions.

**SERVING TIP:** You can serve casabe warm when it's soft and pliable, or allow it to cool and it will harden and have a cracker- like consistency.

# Yuca Fries

**MAKES: 4 servings | PREP TIME: 5 minutes | COOK TIME: 25 minutes**

**Ingredients**

- 3 pounds yuca
- Water
- 3 cups canola oil
- Salt

**Directions**

**Step 1**

Peel your yuca and cut into about 4-inch-long sticks. (I prefer mine closer to a steak fry, but some people like them thinner).

**Step 2**

Place in a pot with enough water to cover the yuca by 1 inch. Bring to a boil and simmer for about 20 minutes, or until the yuca is soft yet still firm enough to hold its shape.

**Step 3**

Drain the water. In a sauté pan or skillet heat the oil over medium heat. Once the oil is hot, place the yuca in the skillet and fry until golden brown, 2 to 3 minutes.

**Step 4**

Place cooked yuca on paper towels to drain the excess oil and serve with Salsa Rosa .

# Yellow Rice

**MAKES: 6 servings | COOK TIME: 30 minutes**

**Ingredients**

- 4 tablespoons achiote oil , fresh or purchased
- 2½ cups rice
- 4½ cups chicken stock
- 2 teaspoons sazón
- Salt

**Directions**

**Step 1**

Heat the oil in a large pot over medium heat. Add rice and cook for a couple of minutes stirring occasionally.

**Step 2**

Pour in the chicken stock, sazón, and salt. You want enough chicken stock to cover all of the rice by 1 inch. Cover and bring to a boil, then reduce heat to low and cook, covered, for another 20 minutes. If the rice is undercooked once all the stock is absorbed, add in a little water, cover, and continue to cook on low until rice achieves desired consistency.

# Avocado and Tomato Salad

**MAKES: 4 servings | PREP TIME: 15 minutes**

This simple salad is elevated with the tropical flavors in this recipe. Avocados are bountiful in Puerto Rico and can be found all over the island, and they lend great taste and texture to many dishes. This salad is perfect for a quick meal with lots of flavor.

FOR THE SALAD

- 2 large tomatoes, sliced
- ½ small red onion, sliced
- 2 avocados, sliced
- 2 tablespoons chopped cilantro

FOR THE DRESSING

- 2 limes, juiced
- 3 tablespoons white vinegar
- 1 tablespoon olive oil
- Salt
- Pepper

TO ASSEMBLE THE SALAD

Layer half of the tomatoes, red onion, avocados, and cilantro on a serving plate. Layer in the other half of the ingredients.

TO MAKE THE DRESSING

Whisk together the lime juice, vinegar, olive oil, salt, and pepper in a small bowl, drizzle over the salad, and serve.

# Avocado and Crab Salad

**MAKES: 4 servings | PREP TIME: 25 minutes**

**Ingredients**

- 1 (8-ounce) can lump crab meat
- ¼ red onion, chopped
- ½ green pepper, chopped
- ¼ cucumber, chopped
- 2 tablespoons chopped cilantro
- 1 lemon, juiced
- 2 tablespoons olive oil
- Salt
- Pepper
- 2 avocados

**Directions**

**Step 1**

In a large bowl toss together lump crab meat, onions, peppers, cucumbers, and cilantro. Add half the lemon juice, olive oil, salt, and pepper. Cover and refrigerate until ready to use.

**Step 2**

Peel and roughly chop the avocados. Drizzle with a little olive oil, salt, and pepper.

3 . Spoon some chopped avocado into a lightly greased 1-cup measure and lightly press down, then add some of the crab mixture. Slide the mold off and serve. Add a little more chopped cilantro as garnish if you want.

VARIATION TIP: Add a layer of cooked rice between the avocado and crab layers to make this a more substantial, satisfying meal.

# Star Fruit and Prosciutto Salad

**MAKES: 2 servings | PREP TIME: 10 minutes**

Pork and ham (prosciutto, in this recipe) are big parts of Puerto Rican cuisine; you'll see them in everything from appetizers to main courses and side dishes. A star fruit and ham salad is a delicious, easy pairing that has an extra *wow* factor. This is the perfect salad to serve as an appetizer or pair with a nice summer lunch.

FOR THE SALAD

- 1 cup lettuce
- ½ cup arugula
- 4 ounces prosciutto
- 1 thinly sliced star fruit

FOR THE DRESSING

- 1 tablespoon sherry vinegar
- 3 tablespoons olive oil
- ½ teaspoon garlic powder
- Salt

TO ASSEMBLE THE SALAD

**Directions**

**Step 1**

Rinse, dry, and chop the lettuce. Place lettuce into a medium salad bowl and add the arugula on top.

**Step 2**

Roughly chop the prosciutto and place it on top of the arugula, then add the thinly sliced star fruit.

TO MAKE THE DRESSING

In a small bowl whisk together vinegar, olive oil, garlic powder, and salt. Drizzle the salad with dressing and serve.

VARIATION TIP: If you don't like prosciutto, sliced serrano ham will work just as well. Add some thinly sliced bell pepper for extra texture and flavor.

# Cabbage Salad

**MAKES: 4 servings | PREP TIME: 45 minutes**

**Ingredients**

- 3 cups sliced cabbage
- 1½ cups julienned carrots
- 1 roughly chopped avocado
- 2 tablespoons olive oil
- 4 lemons, juiced
- Salt
- Pepper

**Directions**

**Step 1**

In a large bowl, mix together cabbage, carrot, and chopped avocado. Add in olive oil and the juice from the lemons.

**Step 2**

Add salt and pepper to taste, and toss to coat all ingredients evenly. Allow to rest at least 30 minutes to allow flavors to really come through.

VARIATION TIP: Adding a tablespoon of finely chopped cilantro really makes the flavors pop in this salad. If you want to make it a creamy salad you can add ½ cup mayonnaise before tossing it all together.

# Octopus Salad

**MAKES: 4 servings | PREP TIME: 20 minutes**

FOR THE SALAD

- 1 (8-ounce) can pre-cooked octopus
- ½ green pepper, chopped
- ½ red pepper, chopped
- ½ red onion, diced
- 1 small tomato, chopped

FOR THE DRESSING

- 1 tablespoon olive oil
- 1 garlic clove, minced
- 1 tablespoon white vinegar

- ½ lime, juiced
- Salt

I used to make this with fresh octopus and always had a hard time finding it, until one of my friends taught me how to make it with canned octopus instead. Canned octopus is available at most stores now and tastes just as good in this recipe. Worst-case scenario, it's also easy to find online.

TO ASSEMBLE THE SALAD

Drain and rinse the octopus, pat dry, and cut into bite-size pieces. In a large bowl, toss together the octopus, green and red peppers, onions, and tomatoes.

TO MAKE THE DRESSING

In a small bowl whisk together the olive oil, minced garlic, vinegar, lime juice, and salt to taste. Drizzle dressing over salad and toss to coat evenly.

INGREDIENT TIP: If you want to make this with fresh octopus, place it in a pot covered with salted water and bring to a simmer, cover, and allow to cook for about 1 hour. Allow it to cool, then clean and slice before adding to the salad.

# Three-Meat Sandwich

**MAKES: 1 sandwich | PREP TIME: 5 minutes**

**Ingredients**

- 10-inch French bread loaf
- 2 tablespoons ketchup
- 2 tablespoons mayonnaise
- 4 ounces sliced Swiss cheese
- 4 ounces sliced roast pork
- 4 ounces sliced serrano ham
- 4 ounces sliced roast beef
- ¼ cup lettuce, shredded
- 1 sliced tomato

**Directions**

**Step 1**

Slice the French bread loaf in half lengthwise and spread your ketchup and mayo on the inside of the bottom bun.

**Step 2**

Add the cheese, pork, ham, roast beef, lettuce, and tomato. Close sandwich, slice in half, and serve.

VARIATION TIP: Instead of the roast pork, use shredded Pernil , and replace the roast beef with leftover skirt steak from the Jibarito recipe. Try it grilled: Place in a panini press until toasted and serve.

# Cuban Sandwich

**MAKES: 4 sandwiches | PREP TIME: 20 minutes**

**Ingredients**

- 1 Cuban bread loaf
- 4 tablespoons mayonnaise
- 4 tablespoons yellow mustard
- 8 ounces sliced Swiss cheese
- 16 ounces sliced ham
- 16 ounces sliced roast pork
- 4 dill pickles, sliced

**Directions**

**Step 1**

Cut Cuban loaf into quarters and halve each section lengthwise. Spread the mayonnaise and mustard on the inside of each section.

**Step 2**

On each sandwich, layer Swiss cheese, ham, pork, and dill pickle slices. Close up and serve.

VARIATION TIP: Place in a sandwich press and toast until warm and the cheese is melted.

SUBSTITUTION TIP: If you can't find cuban bread, use Italian bread.

# Cheesecake Popsicle

**MAKES: 16 servings | PREP TIME: 4 hours**

**Ingredients**

- 8 ounces cream cheese
- 1 (14-ounce) can sweetened condensed milk
- 1 (12-ounce) can evaporated milk
- 1 cup whole milk
- 1 teaspoon vanilla extract
- 1 teaspoon granulated sugar

**Directions**

**Step 1**

Place the cream cheese, condensed milk, evaporated milk, whole milk, vanilla extract, and sugar in a blender and blend until smooth.

**Step 2**

Pour mixture into Popsicle molds or small plastic cups. Place a Popsicle stick into each mold and freeze for at least 4 hours before serving.

# Nutella Popsicle

**MAKES: 16 servings | PREP TIME: 4 hours**

**Ingredients**

- 1 (13-ounce) jar Nutella
- 1 (14-ounce) can sweetened condensed milk
- 1 (12-ounce) can evaporated milk
- 1 cup whole milk
- 1 teaspoon vanilla extract
- 1 teaspoon granulated sugar

**Directions**

**Step 1**

Place the Nutella, condensed milk, evaporated milk, whole milk, vanilla extract, and sugar in a blender and blend until smooth.

**Step 2**

Pour into Popsicle mold or small plastic cups. Place a Popsicle stick into each and freeze for at least 4 hours before serving.

# Fried Plantains

**MAKES: 6 servings | PREP TIME: 5 minutes | COOK TIME: 15 minutes**

**Ingredients**

- 3 green plantains
- 1½ cups olive oil
- Salt

**Directions**

**Step 1**

Cut the ends off of each plantain. Find one of the ribs that runs lengthwise and slice along it. Using your fingers or a spoon, remove the skin. Slice the plantains into one-inch medallions.

**Step 2**

In a sauté pan or skillet, heat enough olive oil to cover the plantains over medium-high heat. Place plantain slices into heated oil and allow to fry for 2 to 3 minutes on each side. Remove the plantains from the frying pan and place on a paper towel to absorb excess oil and cool.

**Step 3**

Once cool enough to handle, flatten the plantain slices. You can use a tortilla press for this if you have one, or you can use the bottom of a plate, a spatula, or even your hand.

**Step 4**

Place flattened plantains back into the heated oil and allow to fry until they are a beautiful golden brown, for 3 to 4 minutes. Remove from oil and place on a paper towel to cool. Sprinkle with salt before serving.

# Fried Sweet Plantains

**MAKES: 6 servings | PREP TIME: 5 minutes | COOK TIME: 10 minutes**

**Ingredients**

- 3 ripe sweet plantains
- 2 cups oil
- Salt

**Directions**

**Step 1**

Cut the ends off of each plantain. Find one of the ribs that runs lengthwise and slice along it. Using your fingers or a spoon, remove the skin. Slice the plantain into half-inch sections.

**Step 2**

Heat oil in a sauté pan or skillet over medium to high heat. When the oil is hot, place the plantains into the pan and cook until they are golden brown, for 2 to 3 minutes per side. Remove from oil and lay on a paper towel to cool.

**Step 3**

Lightly salt and serve as a snack or with dinner.

VARIATION TIP: For a healthier, no-fry version, bake the sliced plantains at 350°F for 25 minutes until tender.

# Puerto Rican-Style Crab Cakes

**MAKES: 8 patties | PREP TIME: 10 minutes | COOK TIME: 10 minutes**

**Ingredients**

- 2½ tablespoons mayonnaise
- 2 tablespoons Dijon mustard
- 1 teaspoon adobo
- 1 teaspoon sofrito
- 1 teaspoon minced garlic
- ½ teaspoon lemon juice
- 1 beaten egg
- 1 pound lump crab meat
- ¾ cup panko bread crumbs
- 1 tablespoon oil

**Directions**

**Step 1**

In a small bowl whisk together mayonnaise, mustard, adobo, sofrito, garlic, lemon juice, and egg.

**Step 2**

In a medium bowl mix together crab meat and bread crumbs. Fold the mayonnaise mixture into crab mixture, then form 8 patties.

**Step 3**

In a sauté pan or skillet, heat oil over medium to high heat. Add crab cakes to the pan in batches, avoiding crowding, and cook until they are golden brown, for 4 to 5 minutes per side.

STORAGE TIP: These crab cakes will keep in the refrigerator for 3 to 4 days; any leftovers should be frozen.

# Codfish Fritters

**MAKES: 10 fritters | PREP TIME: 5 minutes | COOK TIME: 20 minutes**

**Ingredients**

- 2 cups water
- 1 pound chopped cod fillet
- 2 cups flour
- 1 teaspoon adobo
- 1 teaspoon sazón
- ½ teaspoon baking powder
- ½ teaspoon oregano
- ½ teaspoon cumin
- 2 tablespoons sofrito
- 2 cups oil

**Directions**

**Step 1**

Bring 2 cups water to a boil in a saucepan. Place cod into water and boil for 10 minutes.

**Step 2**

Meanwhile, in a medium bowl whisk together flour, adobo, sazón, baking powder, oregano, and cumin. Once completely combined slowly add in the water and sofrito. You will end up with a thick batter.

**Step 3**

After 10 minutes, remove the cod from the water, pat dry, and fold it into the batter.

**Step 4**

Heat oil over a medium to high heat in a sauté pan or skillet. Drop heaping spoonfuls of batter into the pan and cook fritters until golden brown, for 3 to 4 minutes per side.

SUBSTITUTION TIP: You can also use 1 pound frozen salted cod, which can be found at any major grocery store. Soak the fish in a bowl of water for several hours to remove the salt, then rinse. From here the recipe is the same.

# Sweet Corn Fritters

**MAKES: 15 to 20 fritters | PREP TIME: 10 minutes | COOK TIME: 10 minutes**

**Ingredients**

- 2 cups water
- ½ teaspoon salt
- 1 tablespoon sugar
- 1½ cups cornmeal
- 6 ounces shredded Gouda cheese
- 2 cups oil

**Directions**

**Step 1**

Boil 2 cups water in a medium saucepan. Once at a boil, remove water from heat and stir in the salt, sugar, and cornmeal. Return to heat and cook for 2 to 3 minutes, stirring constantly, until the dough no longer sticks to the pan. Remove from heat and stir in the cheese.

**Step 2**

Once the dough has cooled enough to handle, scoop out 1 heaping tablespoon at a time and roll into a stick shape.

**Step 3**

Heat oil over medium to high heat in a sauté pan or skillet (there should be about 2 inches of oil in the pan). Place formed dough sticks into oil and fry until golden brown, for 4 to 5 minutes. Serve as is or with your favorite dipping sauce.

# Pulled Pork Sliders

**MAKES: 4 servings | PREP TIME: 10 minutes | COOK TIME: 15 minutes**

**Ingredients**

- 2 green plantains
- 6 tablespoons oil
- 1 cup coconut milk
- ½ teaspoon chipotle chili pepper spice (McCormick makes a good one)
- ¼ cup cilantro
- Salt
- 3 cups pulled pork, canned

**Directions**

**Step 1**

Score the plantain lengthwise along one of the ridges, and remove the peel. Slice into 1-inch pieces.

**Step 2**

Heat about 4 tablespoons of oil in a sauté pan or skillet. Fry plantains until they start to brown, roughly 2 minutes. Flip and fry for another 2 minutes, then remove from heat and place on a paper towel.

**Step 3**

Once they're cool enough to handle, smash plantains on a piece of wax paper using the bottom side of a plate to flatten them.

**Step 4**

Heat another 2 tablespoons of oil in the skillet and fry plantains again for 2 minutes per side. Remove plantains and place on paper towels to drain excess oil.

5 . Put coconut milk, chipotle pepper chili spice, cilantro, and salt in a food processor and pulse until smooth and well combined.

6 . Build sliders with shredded pork in between 2 fried plantains. Drizzle each with the chipotle sauce and serve.

SUBSTITUTION TIP: Use leftover Pernil for an even tastier Puerto rican dish.

# Mashed Plantains

**MAKES: 4 servings | PREP TIME: 10 minutes | COOK TIME: 10 minutes**

**Ingredients**

- 2 garlic cloves
- 1 cup plus 1 tablespoon olive oil
- Salt
- 3 green plantains
- 1 cup chicharrónes , homemade or purchased

**Directions**

**Step 1**

Put garlic in a large pilon. Add 1 tablespoon olive oil and salt, and mash until you get an oily paste. Set aside.

**Step 2**

Cut both ends off of the plantains. Find one of the ribs that runs lengthwise and slice along it. Peel the skin off using your fingers or a spoon and slice the plantains into 1-inch pieces.

**Step 3**

Heat 1 cup olive oil over medium to high heat (use enough to cover the sliced plantains in the bottom of the pan). Fry plantains for 2 to 3 minutes per side. Remove from oil and place on a paper towel to cool.

**Step 4**

Add fried plantains and chicharrónes to the pilon and mash together. Once completely combined, scoop out and serve.

VARIATION TIP: Mofongo can be served as a main course with a side of white rice. I have often had it as a side dish drizzled with an Ajillo sauce and plated with churrasco. You can also roll it into small dumpling-like balls and serve in soup. Feel free to use store-bought pork rinds in place of the chicharrónes to save time.

COOKING TIP: While traditionally made in a pilon, most restaurants now use food processors to make Mofongo. This is a perfectly acceptable way to prep this meal and will save you some time and effort.

# Meat-Stuffed Sweet Plantains

**MAKES: 12 pinwheels | PREP TIME: 10 minutes | COOK TIME: 15 minutes**

***Ingredients***

- 3 ripe yellow plantains
- 1 cup vegetable oil
- 1 cup picadillo, fresh (see here ) or canned
- 2 eggs
- Pinch salt

**Directions**

**Step 1**

Cut both ends off of the plantains. Find one of the ribs that runs lengthwise and slice along it. Peel the skin off using your fingers or a spoon. Slice lengthwise; you should have 4 to 5 slices per plantain.

**Step 2**

Heat the oil in a large sauté pan or skillet over medium to high heat. Once the oil begins to sizzle, lay the plantain strips in the skillet and fry for 3 to 4 minutes per side. Remove from oil and roll into small pinwheels, placing toothpicks in the ends so they hold the circular shape. Make sure there is a small hole in the middle for the picadillo filling.

3 . Spoon picadillo into the center of each pinwheel.

**Step 4**

In a small shallow dish beat the eggs with a pinch of salt. Dip the filled pinwheels into the egg and place back in the oil, frying for 3 to 4 minutes. Place pinwheels on paper towels to drain excess oil and let cool before serving.

VARIATION TIP: Add shredded cheese on top of each pinwheel before frying them the second time, letting the cheese melt before serving. I love my picadillo, so I tend to stuff everything with it, but feel free to experiment with different fillings like crab or lobster. This recipe will work with almost any filling and be delicious.

# BBQ Chicken Kabobs

**MAKES: 8 servings | PREP TIME: 2 hours | COOK TIME: 10 minutes**

**Ingredients**

- 4 pounds chicken thighs
- 1 tablespoon adobo, fresh (see here ) or purchased
- 1½ tablespoons sazón, fresh (see here ) or purchased
- 2 teaspoons oregano
- 1 tablespoon olive oil
- ⅓ cup barbecue sauce

**Directions**

**Step 1**

Cut chicken thighs into about 1-inch cubes, and put in a large bowl. Add adobo, sazón, oregano, and olive oil to the chicken. Toss until the chicken is completely coated. Cover the bowl and marinate in the refrigerator for at least 2 hours.

**Step 2**

After the chicken has marinated, remove from the refrigerator. Heat the grill while you place the chicken onto skewers. Lay skewers on the grill and cook until chicken reaches an internal temperature of 165°F. Brush with your favorite barbecue sauce and serve.

VARIATION TIP: I often make pork shoulder kabobs on the grill using a different marinade: 1 tablespoon oregano, 1 teaspoon cumin, 5 minced garlic cloves, ½ cup brown sugar, ⅓ cup orange juice, 2 tablespoons lime juice, and 1 tablespoon light rum. Marinate cubed pork in the refrigerator for at least 2 hours; the rest of the recipe is the same.

# Breaded Steak

**MAKES: 6 servings | PREP TIME: 10 minutes | COOK TIME: 15 minutes**

**Ingredients**

- 3 cups panko bread crumbs
- 2 tablespoons salt
- 2 tablespoons pepper
- 1 tablespoon adobo, fresh (see here ) or purchased
- 1 teaspoon garlic powder
- 2 eggs
- 6 thinly sliced steaks (I use top round)
- Oil

**Directions**

**Step 1**

In a shallow dish whisk together panko bread crumbs, salt, pepper, adobo, and garlic powder. In a second shallow dish beat the eggs.

**Step 2**

Take each steak and press both sides into the bread crumb mixture, then dip in beaten eggs, and back through the bread crumbs a second time. Set aside on a plate.

3 . Add about ½ inch of oil into a large sauté pan or skillet and heat over medium to high heat. Once the oil is hot, add the breaded steaks and fry until the breading turns a nice golden brown, 2 to 3 minutes per side. Remove from the skillet, place on paper towels to drain excess oil, and serve.

VARIATION TIP: These steaks can be served as the main dish with a side of rice and beans or served as a sandwich on a toasted bun with some French fries.

# Caramel Custard

**MAKES: 6 servings | PREP TIME: 8 minutes | COOK TIME: 35 minutes plus 1 hour chill time**

**Ingredients**

- 1¼ cups granulated sugar, divided
- Water
- 1 (12-ounce) can evaporated milk
- 5 eggs
- ⅛ teaspoon salt
- 1 teaspoon vanilla

**Directions**

**Step 1**

Pour ¾ cup sugar and ¼ cup of water into a microwave-safe glass bowl, and stir until the sugar is completely dissolved. Microwave until mixture becomes a golden honey color, 5 to 6 minutes. Watch carefully so as not to let it burn.

**Step 2**

Pour caramel into ramekins and set them in a deep baking dish.

**Step 3**

Whisk together the evaporated milk, eggs, salt, vanilla, and ½ cup of sugar, and divide this mixture evenly among the prepared ramekins.

**Step 4**

Pour water into baking dish about halfway up the ramekins. Bake at 325°F until the flan is set, 20 to 25 minutes. Using tongs or an oven mitt, remove ramekins from baking dish and place in the refrigerator to allow to cool completely, at least 1 hour.

5 . Once cooled, gently run a butter knife between the edge of the ramekin and the flan. Turn the ramekin upside down and slide the flan onto a plate to serve.

COOKING TIP: My brother doesn't like to bake so he microwaves his flan. To do this, complete steps 1 through 3, and then microwave the flan-filled ramekins on high for about 8 minutes with a serving plate over top so they don't overflow. Then cool in the refrigerator as above.

VARIATION TIP: You can use 1 (13.5-ounce) can of coconut milk instead of evaporated milk to make Flan de coco (coconut flan). Top it with a little whipped cream, fruit, or ice cream.

# Coconut Custard

**MAKES: 6 servings | PREP TIME: 2 minutes | COOK TIME: 8 minutes plus 2 hours chill time**

**Ingredients**

- 2 (13.5-ounce) cans coconut milk
- ½ cup cornstarch
- ½ cup sugar
- ¼ teaspoon salt
- Water
- Cinnamon

**Directions**

**Step 1**

Pour coconut milk into a large saucepan. Whisk in cornstarch until mixture is smooth, then add the sugar and salt.

**Step 2**

Heat the coconut milk mixture over medium heat, stirring constantly until the mixture begins to thicken, then remove custard from heat.

**Step 3**

Sprinkle the insides of 6 ramekins with a little cold water, then spoon the custard evenly into the ramekins. (The water helps to keep the custard from sticking to the ramekins.) Cool the custard to room temperature, then place ramekins in the refrigerator to chill for 2 hours.

**Step 4**

Run a butter knife around the edges of the ramekins to loosen custard, then turn it upside down and slide it onto a plate. Top with cinnamon to taste and serve.

FAMILY IS VERY IMPORTANT TO PUERTO RICANS, AND THIS comes across in the meals we eat. Dinner is a time for families to gather together at the end of the day, break bread, and share their experiences. For this reason, one-pot recipes are a huge part of our cuisine and culture—meals that make it easy and inexpensive to feed a lot of people without too much work. In this chapter we will explore some great one-pot and one-skillet recipes that are simple to create and great for feeding the whole family.

# Cheesy Yuca Balls

**MAKES: 20 bolitas | PREP TIME: 5 minutes | COOK TIME: 35 minutes**

**Ingredients**

- Water
- Salt

- 1 pound frozen yuca
- 6 ounces cheddar cheese, cubed
- Pepper
- 2 cups oil

**Directions**

**Step 1**

Fill a large pot with water. Add about 1 tablespoon of salt and bring to a boil.

**Step 2**

Place yuca into boiling water and cook until fork tender, 20 to 25 minutes.

**Step 3**

Drain the water from the yuca and remove the wood stems. Season cores with salt and pepper and mash until they are the consistency of mashed potatoes.

**Step 4**

Take 1 tablespoon at a time of the mashed yuca and place one of the cheese cubes into the center, closing the yuca around the cheese. Repeat with the rest of the yuca.

5 . Heat about 2 cups of oil in a sauté pan or skillet over medium heat. Add the yuca balls and fry until golden brown, 1 to 2 minutes per side. Remove from the skillet and place on paper towels to drain excess oil.

VARIATION TIP: I enjoy the sharp taste of cheddar cheese in these bolitas, but my little brother prefers mozzarella cheese—both work great, and mozzarella melts quicker, making the bolitas a little cheesier.

**ENTERTAINING TIP:** These bolitas are great on their own, but they're even better with Salsa Rosa . You can also make a sweet and savory guava dipping sauce by mixing 2 tablespoons of guava paste with ¼ cup white vinegar; microwave until the paste is completely melted into the vinegar, stir, and serve.

# Corn Dumplings

**MAKES: 8 servings | PREP TIME: 15 minutes | COOK TIME: 1 hour**

***Ingredients***

- 2 cups corn flour
- ¼ teaspoon ground anise
- 1 cup coconut milk
- ½ cup honey
- Banana leaves for cooking (see here for prep)
- Salted water

**Directions**

**Step 1**

In a medium bowl combine corn flour, ground anise, coconut milk, and honey and mix until smooth.

**Step 2**

Cut the banana leaves into roughly 8-by-8-inch squares. Spoon about 2 tablespoons of the corn flour mixture into the center of each leaf. Roll the leaf like a cigar; there should be about 1½ inches on each end of the leaf that has no corn mixture in it. Pinch and roll the ends to seal them, and tie with cooking twine.

**Step 3**

Fill a large pot with salted water (use no more than ½ teaspoon salt) and bring to a boil, then reduce the heat to a gentle simmer. Place the rolled banana leaves into the water and simmer for 1 hour.

**Step 4**

Unwrap leaves and serve.

INGREDIENT TIP: I purchase my banana leaves from a local produce store, but Goya sells pre-packaged, ready-to-use banana leaves if you'd prefer to skip the prep step.

SUBSTITUTION TIP: If you can't find ground anise in your spice aisle, look for ground fennel, which has a very similar flavor profile; while not exactly the same, it will work in this recipe in the small amount needed.

# Puerto Rican Steak Sandwich

**MAKES: 2 sandwiches | PREP TIME: 35 minutes | COOK TIME: 25 minutes**

**Ingredients**

- 1 tablespoon sazón
- 1 teaspoon adobo
- 1½ teaspoon garlic powder, divided
- 1 tablespoon olive oil
- 1 teaspoon white vinegar
- ½ pound skirt steak
- 2 green plantains
- ¼ cup mayonnaise
- ¼ cup ketchup
- Shredded lettuce
- Sliced tomato

**Directions**

**Step 1**

In a large bowl whisk together sazón, adobo, 1 teaspoon of garlic powder, olive oil, and vinegar.

**Step 2**

Trim the fat from the skirt steak and place in the bowl, completely coating it with the marinade. Cover the bowl and allow steak to marinate for at least 20 minutes.

**Step 3**

Cut both ends off of the plantains. Find one of the ribs that runs lengthwise and slice along it. Peel the skin off using your fingers or a spoon. Slice in half lengthwise.

**Step 4**

Heat oil in a large sauté pan or skillet over medium heat, then fry plantain strips for 3 to 4 minutes per side. Remove from oil; while still warm, smash the plantains so you end up with long, wide, flat strips. Place back in the oil and fry for another 2 to 3 minutes per side, then place them on paper towels to drain excess oil.

5 . Drain all but 2 tablespoons of oil from your skillet and return to medium heat. Sear steaks 2 to 3 minutes per side, then remove from skillet and let rest for about 5 minutes.

6 . While steak is resting mix together mayonnaise, ketchup, and ½ teaspoon garlic powder in a small bowl.

7 . To assemble the sandwich, brush mayonnaise mixture on 1 slice of fried plantain. Then layer your steak, lettuce, and tomato, and another fried plantain. Slice in half like a sub and serve with a side of rice.

VARIATION TIP: Add a slice of mozzarella or your favorite cheese to the jibarito to make it even more mouthwatering.

# Puerto Rican Rice with Pigeon Peas

**MAKES: 6 servings | COOK TIME: 40 minutes**

**Ingredients**

¼ cup achiote oil

- 1 cup sofrito
- Salt
- Pepper
- 2 cups white rice
- 2 (15-ounce) cans *gandules verdes* (green pigeon peas)
- 4 cups water
- 3 packets Goya chicken bouillon

**Directions**

**Step 1**

Heat oil in a *caldero* or Dutch oven over high heat until the oil starts to sizzle. Add the sofrito, salt, and pepper and cook, stirring often for about 5 minutes.

**Step 2**

Stir in rice making sure it is evenly coated. Cook for a couple of minutes, then add pigeon peas, water, and chicken bouillon.

3 . Bring mixture to a boil without stirring. Once boiling, stir, lower the heat, then cover and simmer for about 20 minutes.

**Step 4**

Stir rice and serve.

VARIATION TIP: A lot of people add ham or bacon to this dish. If using, add about ½ pound at the same time as the sofrito. You can also add 2 tablespoons chopped pimento olives with the pigeon peas for an extra kick.

# Rice with Chicken

**MAKES: 6 servings | PREP TIME: 5 minutes | COOK TIME: 1 hour 5 minutes**

***Ingredients***

- 2 tablespoons olive oil
- 2 pounds chicken thighs
- ½ cup diced onion
- ¼ cup chopped green olives
- ½ cup sofrito
- 2 tablespoons capers
- 1 (12-ounce) can tomato sauce
- 2 cups white rice, uncooked
- 4 cups water

**Directions**

**Step 1**

Heat oil in a *caldero* or Dutch oven over high heat. Place chicken thighs into heated oil and cook for 4 to 5 minutes per side, just enough to brown the chicken but not cook all the way through. Remove chicken from caldero and set aside.

**Step 2**

In the caldero, add diced onions and cook until they soften and start to become translucent, about 5 minutes. Add olives, sofrito, capers, and tomato sauce; mix together and cook for another 5 minutes.

**Step 3**

Reduce heat to low and add in the rice and water, then place the chicken back in. Simmer for 20 minutes, stir, then cover, simmering for another 25 minutes.

COOKING TIP: You might feel the need to stir the rice as it cooks. Resist this urge! Stirring your rice while it cooks will make it too sticky.

VARIATION TIP: Traditionally this was made with bone-in chicken thighs, which is how my dad and his family cooked it. I have always used boneless thighs. If you use bone-in, they should be tender enough by the time they finish cooking to easily pull the meat away from the bone with a fork.

# Rice with Sausage

**MAKES: 6 servings | PREP TIME: 10 minutes | COOK TIME: 50 minutes**

**Ingredients**

- 3 tablespoons sofrito
- 2 teaspoons sazón
- 2 (5-ounce) cans Vienna sausage
- 2 (8-ounce) cans tomato sauce
- Salt
- ¼ cup olive oil
- 3 teaspoons alcaparras (capers)
- 2 cups white rice
- 1¾ cups water

**Directions**

**Step 1**

Add sofrito, sazón, sausages plus their liquid from the cans, tomato sauce, salt, oil, and *alcaparras* to a large caldero or Dutch oven. Bring to a simmer over low heat, then add in rice and simmer for another 5 minutes.

**Step 2**

Pour the water into the caldero. Bring to a boil, then stir, scraping the rice from the bottom of the pot to prevent burning. Cover the pot and reduce the heat to low and simmer for about 20 minutes.

**Step 3**

Uncover and stir rice again, making sure no rice is sticking to the bottom, recover, and cook for another 10 minutes. Remove from heat and let rest, covered, for 5 minutes before serving.

VARIATION TIP: I have a few friends who also like to put kidney beans in this dish. Try serving your Arroz con Salchichas with the Plátanos Maduros .

# Pot Roast

**MAKES: 8 servings | PREP TIME: 15 minutes | COOK TIME: 2 hours 30 minutes**

**Ingredients**

- 4½ tablespoons olive oil, divided
- 2 tablespoons white wine vinegar
- 1½ tablespoons adobo
- 1 teaspoon oregano
- 3 pounds round or chuck roast
- 1 cup cubed ham
- ⅓ teaspoon garlic powder
- 3 chopped onions
- 1 cup cooking sherry

- 2 cups water
- Salt
- Pepper
- 2 chopped carrots
- 2 potatoes, peeled and chopped

**Directions**

**Step 1**

Combine 2 tablespoons olive oil, 2 tablespoons vinegar, 1 tablespoon adobo, and oregano in a small bowl.

**Step 2**

Using a long knife make a slice in the center of your roast. Place the roast in a large bowl or baking dish and coat evenly with the marinade. Rest for at least 15 minutes.

**Step 3**

In a large caldero or Dutch oven, heat ½ tablespoon oil over medium heat. Add in ham, garlic powder, ½ tablespoon adobo, and onions, and sauté about 5 minutes. Remove sautéed ingredients from pot, and stuff them into the slit you made in the roast.

**Step 4**

Heat 2 more tablespoons oil in your caldero over medium heat. Place roast in heated oil and sear on all sides. Pour sherry and water into the pot and season with salt and pepper to taste. Cook, uncovered, until the liquid starts to steam, then turn down to low heat, cover the pot, and simmer for about 2 hours, checking the liquid levels often. Add water if needed. With about 25 minutes left, mix in the carrots and potatoes, then serve.

**SERVING TIP:** Arroz Amarillo is the perfect side for this dinner.

VARIATION TIP: You can replace the cubed ham with about ¼ pound of cooked chorizo.

# Creole Shrimp Stew

**MAKES: 8 servings | PREP TIME: 5 minutes | COOK TIME: 25 minutes**

**Ingredients**

- 3 tablespoons achiote oil
- ¼ cup sofrito
- 3 bay leaves
- ½ cup alcaparrado
- 3 ounces cubed ham
- 1 (16-ounce) can whole peeled tomatoes, drained and chopped
- 1 cup tomato sauce
- 2 pounds medium shrimp, peeled and deveined
- Salt

- Pepper

**Directions**

**Step 1**

Heat achiote oil in a large pot over medium heat. Add the sofrito, bay leaves, alcaparrado, and ham, and sauté for 2 to 3 minutes. Set aside.

**Step 2**

Drain the whole tomatoes and roughly chop them. Add the  tomato sauce and chopped tomatoes to the same pot and return to heat, bringing to a boil.

**Step 3**

Reduce the heat to medium and add the shrimp, cooking for about 5 minutes until they become pink and opaque. Add salt and pepper to taste, cook for a couple of minutes to meld the flavors, then serve.

# Codfish Stew

**MAKES: 8 servings | PREP TIME: 15 minutes | COOK TIME: 1 hour**

**Ingredients**

- Salted water
- ½ pound peeled yuca
- 1½ pounds cod fillet
- 1 tablespoon olive oil
- 2 tablespoons  sofrito
- 1 cup diced onion
- 1 green pepper, diced
- ½ cup tomato sauce
- 1 tablespoon  sazón
- ½ cup pimento stuffed green olives

**Directions**

**Step 1**

Fill a large pot with salted water (use no more than ½ teaspoon salt) and bring to a boil. Place peeled yuca and deboned cod fillets into the water and boil for 35 to 40 minutes.

**Step 2**

Drain the water, then break the codfish into bite-size chunks and chop the yuca into about 1-inch cubes.

3 . Heat olive oil in a large pot over medium heat. Once the oil starts to sizzle, add in the sofrito and sauté for about 1 minute until it becomes fragrant. Then add onions and green pepper, and cook for about 5 minutes until they become tender. Add tomato sauce, sazón, olives, cod, and yuca. Reduce heat to low, cook for 15 minutes, then serve.

**SERVING TIP:** The Guanimes are a perfect side for this dish, or you can serve it over white rice with some Tostones for dipping.

VARIATION TIP: Classic salted codfish is used for this recipe. I tend to make it with fresh cod, but if you are going with salted, make sure to soak in water for a day to remove the salt. You will want to change the water out a couple of times during that period. You can also easily use potatoes in place of yuca if you like.

# Mofongo Stuffing

**MAKES: 8 servings | PREP TIME: 15 minutes | COOK TIME: 35 minutes**

**Ingredients**

- 1 tablespoon plus 1 cup olive oil
- 1 onion, chopped
- 4 garlic cloves, chopped
- ½ cup chopped ají dulce peppers
- 1 ají caballero pepper, chopped
- 2 medium tomatoes, chopped
- 2 tablespoons butter
- 1 cup water
- 4 green plantains
- 1 ounce chicharrónes

**Directions**

**Step 1**

Preheat your oven to 375°F. Heat 1 tablespoon oil in a sauté pan or skillet over medium heat and add onion, garlic, and peppers, and sauté for 5 minutes until the vegetables begin to soften. Add in tomatoes, butter, and 1 cup of water. Bring mixture to a boil, then reduce heat and simmer for 10 minutes, stirring occasionally.

**Step 2**

Let mixture cool slightly, then transfer to a food processor and blend until smooth.

**Step 3**

Cut both ends off of plantains. Find one of the ribs that runs lengthwise and slice along it. Peel the skin off using your fingers or a spoon. Slice the plantains into 1-inch sections.

**Step 4**

Heat about 1 cup olive oil over medium to high heat. Place plantain slices into heated oil (use enough oil to cover the plantains) and fry for 2 to 3 minutes per side. Remove from pan and place on a paper towel to drain excess oil and cool.

5 . In a large bowl combine vegetable mixture, fried plantains, and chicharrónes, mashing it like you would potatoes. Transfer to a baking dish and bake for about 15 minutes. Remove from oven, let cool, and serve.

SUBSTITUTION TIP: If you can't find some of the peppers listed above you can use sweet Italian peppers in place of ají dulce peppers, and while habanero peppers have more heat, you can use a small one or a fresno pepper in place of the ají caballero pepper. See here for a chicharrónes recipe, but in a pinch, you can use pork rinds.

# Sweet Bread Rolls

**MAKES: 10 rolls | PREP TIME: 3 hours | COOK TIME: 30 minutes**

**Ingredients**

- ½ cup warm milk
- 1½ cups warm water
- 1 (¼ ounce) package dry yeast
- 8 egg yolks
- ¾ cup granulated sugar
- 1 cup (2 sticks) melted butter
- 6½ cups bread flour
- 1 teaspoon salt
- Powdered sugar

**Directions**

**Step 1**

Pour milk, water, and dry yeast into a large bowl and let rest for 1 to 2 minutes. The mixture will form a foamy head as the yeast activates.

**Step 2**

While this liquid mixture is resting, in another large bowl whisk together the eggs, sugar, and butter until completely combined. Pour the yeast mixture into your egg mixture and whisk until combined.

**Step 3**

Add in your flour and salt, and knead the dough. If you have a stand mixer with a dough hook, you can use this instead of kneading by hand. You want to knead it until it is tacky. Transfer to a bowl, cover with a kitchen cloth, and rest on the counter for about 2 hours. By the time it's ready it should have doubled in size.

**Step 4**

Lightly flour your working area and place the dough on it. Sprinkle dough with a little flour as well. Break the dough into 10 equal pieces and roll them out into long cords, about ½ inch thick. Coil the cords into circular buns, tucking the end of the cord under the bottom. Place rolls onto a parchment-lined baking sheet, cover, and rest for 45 minutes.

5 . Preheat your oven to 350°F. Lightly brush each roll with a little melted butter and bake for 20 to 25 minutes. Remove from the oven and let buns cool to room temperature, then sprinkle with powdered sugar and serve.

COOKING TIPS: You want your water and milk temperatures to be between 120° F to 130° F.

This is important; if they're too cool the yeast won't rise, if they're too hot you'll kill the yeast. I have done the latter many times while learning to cook with yeast. If kneading by hand, it's important not to overwork the dough as kneading it too much can overheat the yeast. Instead of letting the dough rest on the counter, you can refrigerate it overnight while it rises.

SUBSTITUTION TIP: If you don't have access to bread flour, you can use all-purpose flour.

# Meatloaf

**MAKES: 6 servings | PREP TIME: 10 minutes | COOK TIME: 1 hour**

**Ingredients**

- 1½ cups bread crumbs
- ½ teaspoon cumin
- ½ teaspoon coriander
- 1 teaspoon sazón
- 1 tablespoon adobo
- 2 eggs
- 2 tablespoons sofrito
- 2 tablespoons ketchup
- 2 tablespoons chopped cilantro
- ¼ chopped onion
- 2 pounds ground beef

**Directions**

**Step 1**

Preheat your oven to 350°F. In a large bowl whisk together breadcrumbs, cumin, coriander, sazón, and adobo.

**Step 2**

Add in eggs, sofrito, and ketchup, and combine. Then add cilantro and onions, mixing until completely incorporated. Lastly, add in the ground beef. (This is added last so the beef doesn't get overworked and the meatloaf stays tender.)

**Step 3**

Once the mixture is completely incorporated, place it on a baking sheet and form into a loaf shape. Pour about ½ cup of water onto your sheet pan and bake for 45 minutes to 1 hour. Remove from the oven and serve while hot.

# Plantain Lasagna

**MAKES: 6 servings | PREP TIME: 15 minutes | COOK TIME: 40 minutes**

**Ingredients**

- 5 ripe yellow plantains
- Oil

- 4 beaten eggs
- 2 cups  picadillo
- 1½ cups shredded mozzarella
- 1½ cups shredded Swiss cheese

**Directions**

**Step 1**

Preheat your oven to 350°F. Cut both ends off of the plantains. Find one of the ribs that runs lengthwise and slice along it. Peel the skin off using your fingers or a spoon, then slice lengthwise, ending up with 4 strips per plantain.

**Step 2**

Heat the oil in a large sauté pan or skillet over medium heat. Carefully lay the plantain strips in the oil and fry for 3 to 4 minutes per side. Place on paper towels to drain excess oil.

**Step 3**

Line the bottom of a 9-by-13-inch baking dish with half the fried plantains. Pour half of the egg wash over the plantains making sure to coat them evenly. Spoon the picadillo over the  egg, then evenly spread half of each cheese over the picadillo. Layer the rest of the plantains and egg wash, and top with the remainder of the cheeses. Bake for 20 to 25 minutes until the cheese is completely melted.

SUBSTITUTION TIP: Mozzarella and Swiss are my favorites, but you can use any cheese you like on this one.

# Cream Cheese Turnovers

**MAKES: 9 pastries | PREP TIME: 10 minutes | COOK TIME: 15 minutes**

***Ingredients***

- 1 sheet thawed puff pastry
- 1 (8-ounce) package cream cheese
- ¼ cup granulated sugar
- 1 teaspoon vanilla
- 1 beaten egg white
- 1 tablespoon honey

**Directions**

**Step 1**

Preheat your oven to 350°F. On a lightly floured surface, lay out the thawed puff pastry sheet. Using a pizza cutter or knife, cut into 9 equal pieces.

**Step 2**

In a small bowl whip together cream cheese, sugar, and vanilla. Scoop about 1 tablespoon of the cheese mixture into the center of each pastry. Fold each corner inward so they overlap over the cheese.

www.ingramcontent.com/pod-product-compliance
Ingram Content Group UK Ltd.
Pitfield, Milton Keynes, MK11 3LW, UK
UKHW061706190726
13853UKWH00008B/2426

9 798502 492683